Ivan Fedotov, a Russian pastor who spent eighteen years in Soviet prisons, says he believes the new freedoms in the former Soviet Union could be "short," and soon "great darkness will return."

The window may be closing even as you read . . .

WINDOW IN TIME

Filling the Vacuum of Spiritual Hunger
Left by Communist Rule

Tom White
With Don Tanner

Living Sacrifice Books
Bartlesville, OK

Bible quotations are taken from the New International Version, except as otherwise noted.

A Window in Time

© 1991 by Tom White

Published by Living Sacrifice Books, P.O. Box 2273 Bartlesville, OK 74005

Library of Congress Cataloging-in-Publication Data
White, Tom, 1947-
    A window in time : filling the vacuum of spiritual hunger left by communist rule / Tom White with Don Tanner.
        p.   cm.
    Includes bibliographical references.
    ISBN 0-88264-301-0
    1. Persecution—Communist countries. 2. Evangelistic work—
Communist countries. 3. Communist countries—Church history—
1945- . 4. Church and state—Communist countries. I. Tanner, Don.
II. Title.
BR1608.C7W45 1991
270'.09171'7—dc20   91-14479
                                                    CIP

Printed in the United States of America.

TO
My children,
Dorothy and Daniel.

When the comfortable religious
world around you offers you
its sugar, may you continue
to reach for the salt.

Contents

Contents

Acknowledgments

I am deeply grateful for the directors and workers of the many missions around the world founded by Pastor Richard Wurmbrand. I am proud to march with you. I remain your servant.

A special thank you also to the workers of the Seamen's Christian Friends Society who have worked with us and to the many "nameless" Christians around the world who open their hearts and simply make themselves available to serve Him.

Thanks also to Don Tanner and Joette Whims who faithfully and skillfully assisted me with the writing of this book.

The most important place for our names ever to appear or to be known is in the Lamb's Book of Life.

Part 1

Searching
for Crumbs

1

Looking Through the Window

Two men climb quietly aboard a large Chinese ship anchored in Rotterdam, Holland. Moving through the narrow hallways, they tap on doors giving illustrated Chinese Bibles and New Testaments to the crew.

At one door they meet a smiling face and are invited into the cabin. Prayerfully using pictures, Scriptures and gestures, they explain the gospel to the sailor. His heart is opened. Accepting Christ, he wants to be baptized. But how?

That night at 10 p.m., he locks his cabin door and with pleading eyes asks the two Dutch Christians to baptize him. It is impossible to take him to a church, and soon the ship will leave. Kneeling on a towel in his room, he waits expectantly. The two Christians pour a large container of water over his head and shoulders. Later that night, three more seamen receive Christ . . .

In the African port of Mombassa, two lanky, dark brown seamen with shiny black hair quietly pack their secret cargo among their belongings. Soon their ship would be sailing the Black Sea to Odessa in the Ukraine. Their cargo, a gift of Bibles from an Anglican vicar, would be safe until their arrival.

Later, from their cabin portholes, the Indians study the security on shore at Odessa and note that the bags of each arriving sailor are being carefully searched on the dock. In their room they tear the hard covers off the Bibles, then tie the Scriptures around their ankles with cords.

While officers scour their belongings, the seamen continue to pray silently. An agent looks curiously at them. Did he notice a bulge around their ankles? Tense, the sailors meet his gaze. Suddenly, his attention is diverted, and another officer waves them through the check point. The sailors successfully enter the city.

Searching for a church proves to be a long, hot task, and they begin to despair. It is not Sunday, and they find it difficult to locate a church building. Finally, they see one. Coming closer, they discover with delight a service in progress. They boldly enter through the front door and find themselves in the middle of a Ukrainian wedding.

The families are standing in line to congratulate the wedding couple. The quick-thinking Indians take their place in the line. When their turn comes, they give the bride and groom a Bible.

The newlyweds are shocked. The festivities stop.

The news passes quickly around the room, and delighted guests crowd around them. Suddenly, to their great surprise, the two sailors are lifted into the air as the rejoicing people carry them around the room . . .

Two "port missionaries" climb aboard a Romanian ship docked at a port in England. It is night and the crew is asleep. Only a couple of officers are standing duty.

The captain greets the visitors warmly, an unusual welcome considering the severely controlled history of Romania. They hold out Bibles for the captain. Delighted, he takes one for himself, flips a switch and begins to talk on the ship's intercom system.

The visitors wonder who he is calling — and what he is saying. Soon the entire crew, rubbing sleep out of their eyes, pour through different doors. Dressed in their best uniforms, they begin to line up on the foredeck.

Looking pleased with himself, the captain eagerly introduces the visitors to each man. At first the sailors are not happy being awakened and made to dress in uniform, but their eyes widen with joy as they each receive a Bible . . .

On the island of Fiji in the South Pacific, a large white Russian cruise ship docks. In a small restaurant not far from the dock, the amazed crew sees Russian Bibles on a table. The owner of the restaurant allows them to come in and out all day to secretly "steal" them. And whenever the ship is in port, the sailors return to the restaurant for more of these life-giving books.

The Bibles have not been left on the table by accident. They have traveled from a Hans in Germany to a Merv in Australia to the restaurant owner in Fiji to hungry hearts at sea . . .

In the airport at Lima, Peru, a pilot of Aeroflot Airlines is walking to his flight when a short, muscular Peruvian postal official stands in front of him. He offers the pilot a Bible in Russian.

They cannot speak each other's language. The astounded pilot reaches into his pocket to pull out a large wad of money. The Peruvian Christian stops the pilot with sign language and refuses the money. The Bible is free . . .

Thousands of Eastern Europeans are gathered near the Hungarian border. At three in the morning eight "commuter missionaries" load their vehicles full of Gospels of John in different languages and carry them to a rendezvous point near the border. Wearing official-looking badges and tiny Hungarian flags on their lapels, the team members begin to distribute the life-giving Scriptures among the people.

Assuming the Christian workers are officials, the people readily accept the literature. Within six hours, the team distributes twelve thousand Gospels of John. The day before in another location, they had given away five thousand Gospels.

Wherever they go, they are jostled and pushed as a sea of hands grab for the Scriptures . . .

As I travel around the world, what I witness and hear is nothing less than miraculous. The spiritual hunger and openness to the gospel of Eastern Europeans and the countless other people under Communist tyranny is far greater than we imagine. Christian workers are spreading God's Word wherever they can with overwhelming response.

Filling the Vacuum

The world today is filled with anxiety, fear and crisis. So many nations are in a state of chaos. In every facet of society and in every country of the world, there is political, social, economic, even religious upheaval.

After decades of atheism and Marxist rule, a vacuum exists in the hearts of hundreds of millions behind the curtains of oppression. Multitudes of those who have been part of the faceless Marxist society have rejected the creed of their former Communist masters. They are looking into a new mirror, and it is blank. They badly want to see a face, to have an identity.

During the 1989 Romanian revolution, the people tore the Communist symbols out of their flag. Scenes of huge crowds waving flags with a hole in the center were flashed around the world by the news media. The hole is an invitation to Christians everywhere from millions under the heel of communism looking for the solution to their aimlessness, loneliness, bitterness and frustration. They are searching as never before for answers to the gnawing emptiness in their lives. We must fill this hole with the hope that only Jesus Christ can give.

Searching for the Grail

The Soviet and East European fishing fleet follows the mackerel and other fish around the world in large factory ships, fish carriers and stern trawlers. For twelve years Alan C. has been ministering among the seamen of this large floating mission field which frequently anchors at ports in Scotland.

Often he watches the small boats roar up to the jetty full of men and women from the ships. Many stand in the crowded launches. Their coats flapping in the cool morning breeze, they come to shop in Scotland. As they climb the concrete steps up to the dock and disburse toward the shops, Alan leans against the waterfront railing, waiting for an opportunity to share the gospel of Jesus Christ.

One thing he has noticed: With the ever-changing political situation in Eastern Europe, it is now easier to approach these seamen with a Bible. And their hunger for spiritual reality has never been greater.

On one occasion, Alan met the second mate from a Bulgarian vessel as he was walking briskly back to the small boat landing after shopping. Alan introduced himself and began to share the gospel. The short, olive-skinned seaman promptly put down his packages and invited Alan to sit with him on a nearby bench. The Bulgarian badly wanted to understand what Alan was saying and at one point related his first "Christian" encounter.

"I was in Lisbon," he said with a perplexed look on his face. "We had a free day and as I was walking through the city, I saw a statue of a man standing with his arms stretched out. I stopped to look. He did not have a hard, fighting look on His face like I have seen so many times. He had a different expression."

The second mate paused and gazed out over the water, rubbing his unshaven face. "I found a postcard in a shop near there with a picture of this statue. I bought it."

It was a picture of Christ.

The seaman turned to Alan and smiled proudly. "I put it on the wall above my bed in the ship." He seemed to imply that this was a brave thing to do.

As they continued their conversation, the muscular second mate suddenly crouched over, looked intently at the water and, hand on his chin, spoke of his disaffection with communism. It had ruined his country, he said, and left him with a sense of hopelessness.

Alan invited the man to the Norwegian Seamen's Mission a few blocks away, handing him a small card with a map to the mission on the back. Later that afternoon, the second mate walked into the mission and joined Alan and another Christian who had been on a skiing trip to Bulgaria. As the men talked and sipped coffee together, the sailor asked, "What is the Holy Grail?"

According to medieval legend, the Holy Grail is the cup used by Christ at the Last Supper and thereafter the object of knightly quests. The Grail symbolizes spiritual reality, and today millions of people like this seaman have embarked on a difficult search for it.

The Open Window

Breathtaking changes occur as this book is being written.

The Soviet Union apparently has fallen. New opportunities break open daily. Great civil wars could break out between or within the republics. Wars and rumors of wars we will always have.

Some burning questions for Christians should be: "Are we prepared for ministry?" "Are we available?" "Can we act now?"

The testimonies in these pages continue to present vital lessons on the apostle Paul's command to "be prepared in season and out of season."[1] The

---

[1] II Timothy 4:2.

names of the nations may change but the lessons remain the same.

Among signs of religious revival in the former Soviet Union are increasing numbers of seminarians and the reopening of churches that were used as storehouses, garages and even factories. Bibles are no longer confiscated at some borders, holiday church services are shown on television, public theaters have been screening the dramatic film "JESUS," Christian organizations are conducting massive evangelistic rallies, and religious publications are flourishing.

Christian leaders have been watching Mikhail Gorbachev and Boris Yeltsin as they help to bring about political and religious freedom. Indeed, in the beginning, they seem to have broken the back of hardliners and freed the Soviet people from the tyranny of Stalin. Other Soviet satellite nations have now emerged from under the Russian mantle to seek their own destiny.

Even so, Christians in the former USSR understand that God gives them but a little window in time so they can get the gospel out to all their countrymen. They see the economic and political instability around them.

Ivan Fedotov, pastor of a large unregistered church who spent eighteen years in Russian prisons, said recently that the new freedom in the Soviet Union could be "short." He urges the church in the Free World to make the most of the opportunity because soon the "great darkness will return." This brings into sharp focus what Jesus said, "As long as it is day, we must do the work of him who sent me. Night is coming, when no one can work."[2]

Hundreds of Chinese Christian leaders have recently been arrested. Vietnamese pastors are shot, then their wives receive a bill from the government to pay for the bullet. Iranian pastors are publicly executed in Tehran. The blood of Christ's body — His martyrs — will continue to cry out to us and move us to action.

It is not time to sit back and merely rejoice as the walls of Communist domination seemingly continue to tumble. The greatest wall still stands — the barrier between man and God. Hammers or political change cannot break through that formidable barricade. Only Christ can tear down this wall and create a new identity. The true government is still upon *His* shoulders.

Will the post Communist nations become captive again? What *"ism"* will come after communism? The Godless vacuum will be filling rapidly. Will it be occupied by false religions or materialism, leaving these people even more enmeshed in bitter disappointment? Or will the people discover the path to true freedom?

My purpose for writing this book is first, to give you a fresh look through this window in time at the spiritual hunger of those who have long been under Communist tyranny; second, to enlist you and other committed Christians in the free world to pray for this

---

[2] John 9:4.

great spiritual harvest; and third, to encourage you to become a "fisher of men" — like those whose stories you are about to read.

Not Yet Poisoned

At this moment, hundreds of millions of people who live in Communist lands and in the newly liberated nations have not yet been poisoned by the deceptions of false religions. Like blank sheets of paper, they are waiting for someone to write the gospel message on their hearts.

If we do not write the message, someone else will.

As you read these pages, you will discover how God uses *ordinary* people — like you and me — in extraordinary ways as we make ourselves available to Him to accomplish this task.

2

Ordinary People— Extraordinary Vision

As Mihai's Volkswagen van inched its way closer to the border checkpoint, his heart beat with anticipation. For years this courageous young courier had smuggled gospel literature into captive nations in Eastern Europe. With each crossing, border guards thoroughly searched his vehicle, but they never discovered his secret cargo.

Mihai was an ordinary man whose extraordinary vision was nothing short of challenging. He had no legs. They were amputated almost to his hips. But he was determined not to let this handicap get in his way. He was refitted with metal limbs. And stuffing the literature into the hollow of each leg, he eagerly began his journeys . . .

Most Christians in the West are not encouraged enough to share their faith in Jesus Christ. Tragically, many church leaders believe they must present a pizza party atmosphere to entertain and hold their youth. But underneath the "fun" facade of every believer,

Christ has planted a hunger for commitment, meaning, and dedicated sacrifice.

If we are not soon led into a meaningful outreach for God, our spirit dries up. We must radiate a special vision, or we and those around us will die.

In the coming pages, I want to present you with a challenge that will move you to courageously declare your faith wherever you go.

Feeding on the Crumbs

The Gospel of Matthew records the story of a Gentile woman who came to Jesus with a desperate need. Matthew relates the incident this way:

> The woman came and knelt before him. "Lord, help me!" she said.
>
> He replied, "It is not right to take the children's bread and toss it to their dogs."
>
> "Yes, Lord," she said, "but even the dogs eat the crumbs that fall from their masters' table."

Then Jesus answered, "Woman, you have great faith! Your request is granted."[1]

Today many of us in the West are not aware of how much spiritual bread we possess. Neither do we see the abundance of crumbs under our tables.

My good friend, Mike D. of England, observes how the West is largely hostile, calloused, or indifferent to this abundance: "I remember returning to England after working with Eastern Europeans who had been so hungry for the Word of God. I went

---

[1] Matthew 15:25-28.

breezing into a city park where our church was distributing Gospels. That same week in the East I had given hundreds of Bibles to delighted people. Now, back in England, I wondered what the possibilities were.

"What I experienced quickly reinforced what I already knew. A new kind of intellectual, elite spirit is swiftly rising here which threatens Western Christianity. In his book, *The Wisdom of the Desert*, Thomas Merton writes about Saint Anthony who said, 'A time is coming when men will go mad, and when they see someone who is not mad, they will attack him saying, "You are mad, you are not like us."'[2] Handing out Gospels in the park, I was similarly rejected, looked at strangely and ridiculed. I nearly had the Bibles pushed down my throat. It really made me appreciate the work I had been doing, when I saw how our own people now take the Bible for granted."

"Come" and "Go"

The nations of the West have been blessed with a history of spiritual hunger and revival. Yet we are mystified at our spiritual dryness in the midst of a full variety of church programs. We resort to techniques, seminars and religious formulas, forgetting the simple commands of Jesus:

"Come to me, all you who are weary and

---

[2] Thomas Merton, *The Wisdom of the Desert* (New York: New Directions Publishing Corp., 1960), p. 3.

burdened, and I will give you rest."[3] and
    "Go into all the world and preach the good news . . . "[4]

Come and *go*. Perhaps our bread is getting old and dry because we are not *coming* to our Lord in humble surrender, then *going* to the world in mighty power.

If only we would bend down to look under the table! We would be shocked. For there, around our feet, we would see the men, women and children of the world *coming* — eagerly crawling, hoping to find some spiritual crumbs.

Two thousand people in Moldavia including many non-believers reach for Bibles. There are never enough.

---

[3] Matthew 11:28.
[4] Mark 16:15.

Catching the Vision

Sailors, truck drivers, motorists, and passengers on trains and buses from Eastern Europe and other Communist lands who journey to the West are arriving at our tables as hungry, starving beggars looking for the crumbs. And God is using ordinary people — teachers, students, doctors, office workers, farmers, accountants, construction workers and homemakers — to reach them. These "commuter missionaries" come from Great Britain, Ireland, West Germany, the Netherlands, Australia and other lands. Boldly entering ships, trains, buses, truck stops, concert halls and hotels around the world, they seek the Chinese, Albanians, Cubans, Russians and Eastern Europeans who have developed an intense hunger for God from years of spiritual starvation under Communist rule.

In this book you will be challenged by the heartwarming stories of several missionaries who are sharing Jesus Christ and God's Word with the spiritually famished travelers of the world. You also will observe how they accomplish their mission, and you will learn valuable principles and techniques that will enable you to be more effective in your witness for Christ as well.

Perhaps, like me, you are tired of offering your bread to the spiritually overstuffed, to the cynical and worldly-wise. You too can experience the adventure of sharing your faith with those who are hungry.

Jesus said, "You will receive power when the Holy Spirit comes on you; and you will be my witnesses in *Jerusalem*, and in all Judea and Samaria, and to the ends of the earth."[5]

As you read the thrilling stories of these commuter missionaries, picture how you can share the liberating light of God's love and forgiveness also.

The Myth of Missions

In our time we have created a myth about what it means to be a missionary. Traveling around the world, I often encounter people whose idea of a missionary is one who suffers great privation in a faraway land to preach the gospel to a faraway people. Many of us are so awestricken by this challenge that we ignore the opportunities right around us to share Christ. Because of this, a relatively small number of Christians have discovered the joy of sharing His love and forgiveness with those they meet daily.

Many believers, for example, are dazzled by the glamour and intrigue of smuggling God's Word into Communist lands. I have visited churches, some of whose members have flown to Hong Kong and carried suitcases filled with Bibles across the border into Red China. Some spent thousands of dollars for airline tickets and expenses to carry a few hundred dollars worth of Bibles across the border. But in their own city there may be Chinese — perhaps visiting professors or students — who have never seen a Bible in their life. Who will reach *them*?

On one occasion about thirty Chinese scientists

---

[5] Acts 1:8.

came to our city, right in the Bible-belt of America, to work in various positions in a local company for a year. Christians went to work with them every day. But how many of the Christians stopped to consider this new mission field?

First century followers of Christ believed it was *every* Christian's responsibility to help fulfill our Lord's command to "Go into all the world and preach the good news."[6] This they did, no questions asked, and they reached the entire known world in their generation. Never before had any small body of ordinary men and women made such an impact on the world. But before they went to the "ends of the earth," they "filled Jerusalem" with the gospel.[7]

Many of the encounters of the ordinary people whose extraordinary vision you are about to witness took place in their own "Jerusalems." D.L. Moody, the famous evangelist of the 19th century, said that if the world was going to be reached, it would be done by people of average talent.[8] In this present awakening, once again it is the "ordinary people" who are carrying the light. Imagine yourself now alongside these men and women of "average talent" as they tell you of their incredible encounters in sharing the gospel with those who have never fed on the "crumbs" of God's Word.

---

[6] Matthew 28:18-20; Mark 16:15.

[7] Acts 5:28.

[8] "Colorful Sayings From Colorful Moody," *Christian History*, Issue 25, Vol. IX, No. 1, p. 9.

*This Russian sign says — "Welcome to Scotland!
We have Bibles for you for free!"*

*Eagerly looking at the shore, many of these sailors have been
told by others of the "Biblia" people working in the port.*

We attempt to board a Communist Chinese ship in the Port of Rotterdam, Holland.

ABOVE AND OPPOSITE PAGE: Success! They took all of our special Bible story books printed in Germany.

ABOVE: It was raining, the Russian captain let us set up literature tables inside. The passengers took all 700 Bibles.

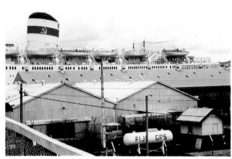

Merv Knight sent Russian Bibles from Australia to Fiji so the Russian sailors could "steal them" from the coffee shop.

We board Soviet tugs in New Zealand.
Soviet freighter in Fremantle, Western Australia.

Part 2

Sharing
the Vision

3

Bread Upon
the Waters

I have long been fascinated by the sea as a carrier of the Good News.

My interest began when I was a high school teacher in Grand Cayman, a British colony south of Cuba. I heard of the sufferings and triumphs of Christians under communism and flew to the United States in the summer of 1972 to learn more about them. I had been reading books written by Richard Wurmbrand and others who had suffered intense persecution and was gripped by their undying faith.

Traveling across America, I was soon challenged by the vision of some Christians who had been dropping Gospels, sealed in plastic packages, off the coasts of China, Albania, and the Soviet Union. From secret drop points, the ocean currents carried these life-giving packages to the beaches of the spiritually hungry.

Returning to Grand Cayman that summer, my life was forever changed. As my flight roared over

Cuba through the established commercial air corridor, I carefully contemplated what I had learned. My Bible lay open on my lap to a passage in the Psalms, which I read and reread with a growing sense of destiny.

> If I take the wings of the morning, and dwell in the uttermost parts of the sea,
> Even there Your hand shall lead me, and Your right hand shall hold me. [1]

What a beautiful, appropriate verse, I mused.

As the airliner left Cuban airspace and seemed to lighten in its descent for Grand Cayman, my thoughts turned toward the island we had just crossed — an island of bondage teaming with hungry masses groping helplessly in their spiritual darkness behind the Sugar Cane Curtain.

I wondered, *Who will penetrate that shroud? Who will lift their burdened hearts?*

I was ready to volunteer. Did the Scriptures not say, "Cast your bread upon the waters, for after many days you will find it again"? [2] The sea would become a carrier of hope. Thinking of the passage I had just read about the "wings of the morning," I realized that the sky too would bring a message of truth.

So began my ministry of distributing gospel literature by sea and by air — an endeavor which eventually resulted in my torturous captivity in a Cuban prison and a broadening of my vision to reach millions around the world under Marxist domination. In recent

---

[1] Psalm 139:9,10 (NKJ).
[2] Ecclesiastes 11:1.

years, I have met other ordinary people who have been challenged by the call to cast their bread upon the waters. These are the missionaries whose fields are the wharfs of the West. Their call is to the ships and fishing vessels of the East. Their mission is to the sailors, merchants and fishermen who are arriving at our tables hungry for the bread of life.

Here, in their own words, are their fascinating stories:

"Why Have You Come?"

I arrived in the evening on a warm spring day as the Chinese ship was dropping anchor in a port on the north coast of Holland. The big gray ship with little stars and waves painted on the bridge slowly eased alongside the pier.

Soon the Chinese were busy mooring the ship, tying the heavy ropes and shouting instructions. I strolled toward them across the dock and stopped silently beside a man directing the activity of his seamen from the quay with gestures and signs. Perhaps an officer, he was about thirty and wore a blue coat, clean pressed trousers and a small cap.

"Yes?" he asked, still watching the ship. "Why have you come?"

Noting his perfect English, I said nothing but showed him a Chinese Bible. He grabbed it from my hand, quickly stuffed it inside his shirt under his coat, then ran to a gravel digger about twenty-five meters away. He tossed the Bible into the giant scoop of the digger, then began walking slowly toward me.

"You must not come on the ship," he cautioned. "The captain will not allow it. Wait in your car." Turning away from me, he said quietly, "I will send them all to see you."

For the next hour I sat in my car with Chinese Bibles and literature laid out next to me on the front seat. The clock seemed to drag as I watched containers filled with sugar being hoisted onto the ship. As night fell, I could hear the horns of other vessels in the distance adding deep tones to the chorus of squeaking cranes lowering the cargo into the ship's hold. Finally, thinking the sailors might never show up, I started to pack the materials.

Suddenly, they began to come. Two by two, a line of men in blue sailor suits stepped down the gangway and strode toward me. Breathing a prayer of thanks, I rolled down my window and began to hand out the literature as one after another the men stopped. I counted thirty-five. Mumbling their appreciation in broken English, they smiled and bowed thankfully. Some paused under lights on the dock to read their Bibles. The man who originally threw the Bible into the digger bent over the big scoop. Retrieving the Bible, he led the other Chinese back to their ship. I drove away, thanking God for what He had been able to accomplish.

—Jan V.

Seeing God at Work

There are seven ports in Holland, with Christian workers like myself spreading the gospel in each. During the past twenty-seven years, I have reached at least a half million seamen with the Word of God.

For twenty-three of those years, I have been saturating Romanian ships with Bibles. Despite opposition from fanatical political police, I think the average Romanian seaman has probably received ten Bibles each from me as their ships return here. And that's not all. Even hymnbooks are popular among the sailors.

One day a Romanian seaman asked, "Can you help us? We want hymnbooks."

I said, "Well, you have the same God I do. Let's pray about it."

After we prayed, I placed a call and located the hymnbooks, but by the time I received them, the ship had left. Several months later, I was looking across the water and saw a small ship approaching the harbor.

Arriving at the dock, I discovered it was the same vessel that had left before receiving the hymnbooks. I asked if my seaman friend was aboard.

"Sorry, but your friend is out," a crewman answered. "Come back tomorrow."

Driving home, I felt a sense of urgency. Deciding not to wait, I gathered up the hymnbooks and rushed back to the ship. Arriving

about 4:30, I found the seaman who wanted them.
He had been on board all the time. He cried for
joy. A half hour later the ship left port. The next
day would have been too late.

—Tom VH

"I Am a Soviet; You Will Give Me One"

Distributing Bibles is a rewarding ministry
for my wife, Nancy, and me. I'd like to tell you
about a couple of incidents that were particularly
heartwarming to us.

One was in a small Scottish fishing village.
Nancy and I were standing outside a newspaper
shop where fishing crews would come in to look
for their mail. We had taken Bibles and New
Testaments out of our shoulder bags for the Russians. After distributing them to several eager
crew members, we heard a heavy stamping noise
behind us.

Turning around, we saw a tall, blond-haired
Russian with heavy seamen's boots and a khaki
smock heading straight for us. As he came closer
we could see the insignia on his shoulders, a patch
with a Russian fishing boat and the letters CCCP
in blue. The big, smooth-shaven sailor marched
straight up to us, clicked his heels, stood at attention and held out his leathery hands.

"I am a Soviet," he intoned. "You will give
me one."

Obviously, someone had told him exactly

what words to say in English. He must have been reciting and practicing them for a long time. Amazed, I placed a Bible in his hands. He looked down at it and smiled happily. Wheeling around, he quickly marched back to the little boat from which he had come.

On the other occasion, a seaman in his fifties from a Bulgarian freezer ship anchored in our harbor in England shuffled toward us wearing what we would call in England a "donkey jacket" with big buttons. His shoes were stretched out and somewhat split at the sides. As he slid his feet along the ground, we could see they were black with dirt.

He had watched us give a Bible to another man, and was delighted when we offered him one as well.

As we walked away, he followed. Wherever we went around town, there he was a short distance behind us. Plump, a little stooped, his black hair streaked with gray, he seemed an unlikely spy. But we began to wonder if someone had sent him to watch us. I didn't like the idea of a spy following us around in England. After all, this is *our* country.

So I said to Nancy, "I'm going to stop and see what he wants."

I stopped in a place where he quickly caught up to us. "Is everything all right?" I asked.

The man simply looked me straight in the

face and spoke in perfect English. "Please, mister, if I pay, can I have one for my friend?"

I was shocked. A Bible was worth several months' wages in his country. Not knowing the price he thought he would have to pay, this man with faded clothing and holes in his shoes was nevertheless willing to give a lot.

While many of us are really not prepared to suffer even a little embarrassment to reach our own friends, he was prepared to pay a high price to buy a Bible for his friend.

From this experience we felt a renewed desire to continue carrying the life-changing message of the gospel to as many as we could.

— David N.

Held Hostage for Bibles

We discovered the ship by accident while driving our little motorbikes in a quiet, secure backwoods area of the docks in a southern England river port. I'm sure Bill saw the vessel before I did, but he wasn't aware of its Romanian registry.

"What do you think?" Bill shouted to me above the roar of our 50cc engines as we shadowed each other back and forth. Slowing down, we gazed intently at the name painted on the bow: *Victoria*. Then, killing our engines and straddling our bikes, we studied the ship more carefully.

The *Victoria* lay tied at the dock still and promising. Although fairly old and battered, the freighter had recently been repainted a deep gray and appeared clean and fresh with its white top. From its stern hung the red, gold and blue flag of Romania. A gangway led from the deck to the landing.

On this hot Sunday afternoon the harbor was quiet. The scent of spices, timber and diesel fuel mingled with the pungent smells of the river. Only the herring gulls wheeling overhead broke the summer stillness. The ship's cargo would not be unloaded until the next day.

With little conversation, we decided to go aboard. We began to unstrap our cases of Bibles which were tied to the luggage racks on the back. I remembered with a smile when Bill's case had fallen into the water and we had to fish it out with a boat hook. We were thankful that it could float for a few minutes. Our cases had compartments for several languages because we never knew what nationality we would encounter on a boat. Also, it was not a good tactic to openly carry the literature in our hands.

We strode across the wharf, stepping around bits and pieces of wood from packing crates and the metal straps that had bound them. Before mounting the twenty steps of the gangway, we said a brief prayer together.

As we stepped onto the gangway, it swung wildly and crashed into the *Victoria's* side with a loud bang. Surely that would bring the crew rushing to inspect their visitors, but the decks remained empty.

I had had only a year and a half experience, but Bill had worked the ships for more than twenty years. So he knew his way around. Bill works with the Seaman's Christian Friends Society, and we at the Wurmbrand Mission supply them and other Christian workers with Bibles.

Checking quickly around the deck, we noticed that no one was in sight. The engines were not running; even the generators seemed silent. We explored the living quarters, walking past the duty officers' cabin and other rooms, and finally stepping through some double wooden doors into the mess room.

Here the whole ship's company, about thirty-five men including officers and crew, was gathered. Off duty, most were watching English television, a rare treat for them. Some were eating. The air was filled with cigarette smoke and the smell of cabbage and fish. The men were casually dressed, wearing light-colored T-shirts or sports shirts. A few, dressed in blue or orange overalls, were dirty from working. We knew many had been subjected to intensive atheistic education all their lives, and we wondered how they would react to us.

Over the previous eighteen months, I had been on many vessels from almost every country in the world. I had never found that first moment

any easier — and I pray that I never will. The first
contact, the first words, are so important in gain-
ing people's attention. The natural fear I feel at
that certain moment makes me dependent on God
for those opening words.

"We are Christians," we began, explaining
who we were and why we had come. Everyone
listened politely. But when the first Romanian
Bible appeared, there was an instant stir in the
room. The television was switched off, and full of
curiosity the seamen crowded around us.

Their attention was riveted on the three or
four Romanian Bibles being passed from hand to
hand. We no longer had to find a way to speak
about the Lord Jesus. Some of them spoke a little
English, and their questions gave us ample opportunity. Most of them had never heard that God had
sent His Son to live and die for them. But they
seemed to know that something was missing in
their lives, and we told them that the Bible could
fill the emptiness. Listening intently, they stood
with sober faces when we shared that this Book
would show them how God in Christ was waiting
to meet their need. Like many Eastern Europeans
with an atheistic upbringing, they longed to read
this Bible.

After handing out the few Romanian Bibles
we carried, we began distributing little booklets
and Gospels. But these were of less interest to
them; they had heard the word "Biblia" in their
own country and were eager for the entire Bible.

Now we had a problem. Opening our cases, we discovered just how little Romanian literature we had. Surprised at finding the ship, we hadn't thought to check the mixture of languages we carried, or we would have replenished our supply of Romanian Bibles before going aboard.

Seeing that there was nothing left in their language, two burly seamen grabbed Bill by the arms. Gently but firmly they sat him in a chair and handed him a hot cup of thick Romanian coffee. Then they explained apologetically in halting English that he would stay there until I came back with Bibles for all of them.

I didn't know whether to laugh or cry. A hostage for Bibles might seem silly to our Western minds, but it was the only way they could think of to make sure I would come back. They were from a country where they were usually lied to, and our promises to return were not convincing. They were absolutely determined to read that Book, and Bill was their "guarantee" that I would keep my word.

Accustomed to the unexpected, Bill calmly drank his coffee, hopeful that I had actually gotten the message. I took my case, scrambled down the gangway and walked briskly back to the motor bikes. Roaring away, I sped to the mission base about five miles away. In the literature room, I emptied my case of the material in other languages, and packed it absolutely full with Romanian Bibles, New Testaments and everything else that I could fit in. I made sure that I had enough Bibles for them all. I had learned a valuable lesson on preparedness.

Within a half hour, I was once again climbing the wobbly gangplank. By the time I reached the mess room, some of the men had gone to their cabins, perhaps to find hiding places for their Bibles. (Their belongings would be searched upon their arrival home.)

Word traveled quickly that I was back with the Bibles, and those who had left returned. Some took an extra copy for their "grandmother" or a friend — or perhaps to sell to Romanian Christians who have contacts with the seamen.

We cannot read every heart, but the Bibles are cherished by the spiritually hungry, whoever they are.

I returned to find a mildly relieved Bill finishing his second cup, deep in conversation with the men standing around his table. We spent a long time sharing the Good News of Jesus Christ with them.

Late on Monday the gray and white *Victoria* lifted anchor and the crew sailed home. We pray that many have received Jesus Christ as their Savior and Lord. These men gave us a unique insight into the hunger of Eastern Europeans for the Word of God.

I started working with ships out of curiosity. Someone came to our church one Sunday to show slides of the dock work, and I decided to visit ships with him for an afternoon just to see what it was like. After working with him for a half day, I was hooked. Occasional dramatic incidents of spiritual hunger like the one we had on the *Victoria* have increased my desire to deliver God's Word.

—John R.

Hunger in the Shetland Islands

Our mission coffee shop in a Shetland Islands port north of Scotland is a lighthouse to the sailors of Eastern Europe. It is a place for weary off-duty seamen to gather for conversation, softdrinks and quiet music. Occasionally, a Russian will play on a small organ we have in the corner of the room. But the center of attraction is the literature table. Here is where these travelers find rest for their souls.

One afternoon, a Russian woman — a cook from a ship — bustled into the mission house with a group of men. Short and stout, she filled out her red and green dress well. She hovered around the men in a motherly way, looking quite the part with her black hair tightly swept back in a bun.

Marching up to the book table, the crew mother busily began to straighten the materials left in disarray by others browsing through the literature. She sent one man across the room for coffee.

But it was obvious she wasn't at the table

simply to organize it. Placing the materials in order, she carefully selected some literature and stuffed it in her bag. Tramping over to us, she described with signs and stumbling words a picture book of the illustrated life of Jesus. Our supply of the book was gone that day, we explained.

But she was determined. Peering intently at us, she asked if we would have this children's literature when she returned next week.

This is a familiar scene as men and women from ships in port visit our coffee house.

As glasnost began to reduce some fear in 1989-1990, the demand for Bibles was so great that we could distribute only the New Testament on the street; then we would give the whole Bible to the travelers later if they came to the mission. In just one month in this fishing village we gave out many Gospels, salvation booklets, New Testaments and more than one thousand Russian Bibles. We could have used thousands more.

Many of the sailors would return to the mission before they left port to express their gratefulness. On the table they placed cigarettes, icons, picture postcards, a model sailing boat, books on Leninism, Russian "grandmother" dolls, and a few other treasures as tokens of their gratitude.

There is something very powerful in the Word of God. A young man named Sasha gave us a poignant example.

He had been in conversation with another Christian in the mission coffee shop. On one occasion she had said to him in Russian, "God bless you." To Sasha this was more than a kind expression.

Since I wasn't in the mission at the time, he wrote me a note, which I had translated.

"This lady says she wants to bless me," he wrote. "But she does not explain to me at what time. When is she going to do this?"

Realizing that he thought the "blessing" was a special thing that could change his life, we felt convicted. Here God had given us a tremendous power, and this man with his spiritual hunger wanted to be part of what we were doing.

He did not want empty, religious sounding words. In Hebrew the word "word" does not exist. The term that is used is the "davar" — the "real thing." Sasha hungered for an encounter with the real thing — God. He would probably rather that we shut our mouths than to give him useless phrases.

Certainly we couldn't take Sasha's question lightly, and with renewed courage, we continued to distribute the Word of God.

— Alan C.

Ports of the World

In 1920 Lenin told his comrades, "Our destiny depends on water transportation."

Since 1945 the USSR has built a formidable

Richard and Sabina Wurmbrand pictured with "port missionaries" who give Christian literature to those on Chinese, Yugoslavian, and Czechoslovakian ships coming to the port of Vancouver, British Columbia.

fleet to dominate the trade routes of the world. In 1939 the Soviet fleet consisted of just 699 vessels, mostly of old construction, small, and concerned with trade only around their own coasts. By 1970 the fleet had grown to 5,900 ships, and by 1980 to 8,300 ships of all types and with the latest in technology. Now in the 1990s, Soviet vessels are to be found in virtually every part of the sea.

So reaching seamen for Christ is not limited to

the ports of Western Europe. This is a worldwide ministry reaching the crews of ships from many lands on every continent. Going to their countries as missionaries, we would find it difficult and dangerous to openly proclaim the gospel. Yet the travelers are coming to us — to our countries, to our towns, to our homes, indeed to our very tables — searching, always searching.

And not only by sea are the hungry people of the world arriving. They are reaching us by trains, trucks, and buses as well.

4

On the Tracks
of Vienna

Let me take you to one of the most unique cities in the world—Vienna. With its back to the Alps and the West, it faces the Eastern steppelands and dominates the banks of the Danube River. Vienna was built at a point where two main routes of trade and tribal migration crossed. Once the heart of an empire that touched most of the known world, this grand imperial city overflows with a rich history of culture and romance.

Here you can stroll down streets lined with stately facades, historical palaces, and tall, modern buildings like the United Nations city. You can drop in to savor the atmosphere of a coffeehouse or browse in a shop overflowing with quality Western goods made in the factories which ring the city. You may visit museums filled with instruments played by great composers, hear *The Magic Flute* performed by the Viennese Volksoper or listen to the Viennese Boys Choir. Then you can climb the 345 steps of the south steeple of St. Stephen's Cathedral to view the magnificent scene of the heart of town. And when dusk falls, you may retire to the Schwarzenberg Palace made over as a grand hotel.

Vienna is the confluence of the Germanic and Slavic civilizations. Built on an extensive plain near the frontier of Czechoslovakia and close to the Hungarian border, the grand city is the spoke from which roads and railways radiate through Eastern Europe. On any sunny day, tourists pour off trains and buses to visit. You can see Middle Eastern women swathed in black wandering down spotless streets, troops of schoolchildren in orderly lines discovering Viennese museums, and tourists from every Eastern European country filing through bustling shops. The streets ring with thirty or more languages. Guests from every level of society have come to taste the sweets from the honeypot of Vienna.

While these tourists are shopping and relaxing, they are reachable and responsive to the gospel of Jesus Christ. Into this unique situation, God has called men and women from the West to share His Word.

Many opportunities to distribute Bibles, Scripture portions and gospel literature come through the East European trains that stop in Vienna. Train compartments often are jammed with travelers, their luggage packed with more items gathered in the West. People move in and out of their seats, pulling cases through windows to get them on board or rearranging their piles of belongings. Crowds of tourists block the gangways and fill the aisles.

Certainly, the confusion does not create the ideal situation to offer them God's Word. But this is the only opportunity "train missionaries" get. And we know the travelers spend hours poring over the literature they receive because they have nothing else to read during the long journey home.

So the teams get through the compartments the best they can. The stories of their experiences sound like excerpts from a high adventure thriller. Here, in the words of just a few of these "train missionaries," is an exciting glimpse into the evangelism taking place on the tracks of Vienna:

Tucked Safely in Their Bags

When one of our team members boards a train, he never knows what he will encounter or the lives he will touch.

One day, I had a few minutes to sit in one of the little compartments before the Hungarian-Romanian train left Vienna. I slipped into a seat beside an elderly woman sitting alone.

Leaning across the aisle, I handed her a Gospel. Immediately, her eyes lit up. I dug through my bag and found a little Hungarian book and gave that to her, too. Again, her face showed her gratitude.

In halting English, she explained that she was a retired school mistress. Since she lived on a small pension, she had saved very hard so she could come away for the weekend to buy some goods in the shops of Vienna. From her bearing and speech, I could tell she was a sensitive, cultured woman.

"Do you have a Bible?" I asked.

She shook her head so I gave her one along with a book by Joni Eareckson Tada, a handicapped American author with an inspiring testimony. The elderly woman was thrilled, almost tearful, as she accepted my gifts.

Tucking the books into her bags, she rummaged through her luggage and pulled out a packet of English Earl Grey tea. I knew that East Europeans love imported English tea so much that they try to buy some each time they come to the West, although it costs them quite a bit in their currency. She eagerly offered me the small packet.

My heart was thrilled with her generosity and happiness, but I gently refused her gift and rejoiced with her for the few minutes we had left together.

Many times, we encounter unusual situations that touch us deeply. One of the Irish girls on my team had such an experience.

She was giving out Scriptures on a train when she came to a compartment and met a handsome young man. She quickly noticed he had no hands. Cautiously, the girl offered him some literature, not sure how he would react.

He eagerly held out both arms and accepted the books. His apparent desire to receive the literature moved her deeply. Another evening, our team arrived at the south station in Vienna. The night before, the trains had been thinly populated so we had prayed earnestly about tonight's excursion.

With only one train waiting, the platform looked almost deserted. We glanced at each other, wondering if we would have another poor night.

Then we noticed two coaches in the middle of the train jammed with children returning to Poland with their teachers. The students, all in uniforms, hung out every window, laughing, talking and making a lot of noise. They looked about twelve or thirteen years old.

Instead of boarding the crammed coaches, we walked alongside the train, handing out little booklets and gospels, New Testaments and Bibles in Polish, and an assortment of other books and items. The children were excited, happily reaching out to pull their gifts into the coach.

Suddenly, a harsh voice shouted. Every head quickly popped back inside the carriages. In an instant, no one was in sight.

I didn't want to lose this God-given opportunity to give these children His Word, so I climbed the steps between the two carriages to confront the person giving the orders. Several of my companions followed.

Inside, I met two women sitting beside the door. Opening my bag, I showed them what I had.

With silent prayer, I asked the first woman, evidently a teacher, "Will this be all right?"

A smile spread over her face. The friendly

Polish nun sitting beside her nodded. Evidently, the angry nun who had shouted, "No, no, no!" had left the coach.

The teacher called out two names. Two school monitors stepped up before us with arms out-stretched. We piled Bibles, New Testaments and children's literature on their willing arms. The students then distributed the books throughout the two carriages to eager boys and girls.

The English-speaking teacher said, grate-fully, "We will make sure the children put the books safely in their bags."

After we stepped back onto the platform, the train pulled out. The windows were filled with dozens of hands waving goodbye to us like little white flags.

— Brian L.

The Special Compartment

Each "train missionary" learns early in his ministry that he faces certain risks. Before the fall of Ceausescu, the risks on Romanian trains often were the greatest.

I had a harrowing experience on one. I knew that most trains wait for two hours before pulling away to Bucharest. So two of us would come to the station early. One would stay on the platform contacting boarding passengers, while the other distributed literature inside.

On this particular day, it was my turn to board the train. Carrying Russian, Romanian and Bulgarian literature in my blue shoulder bag, I greeted people along the corridor and between the compartments, asking them in which language they would like to receive the gifts I handed them. I slowly worked my way through the six long cars of the train.

Each little compartment held six people. Once in a while, I could see inside. But usually the door was closed and a brown curtain covered the glass walls.

After knocking, I entered the compartment to hand out literature. Sometimes the seats would be filled with men only, other times with families or tourists. Most of the people would be smoking, drinking cokes or eating bananas bought in the West. Their handbags and luggage littered the floor.

When I discovered a family, I would distribute children's Bibles. Each time, I watched the children's and parents' faces. The boys would be reluctant to take the books, but the girls were delighted with their gifts.

When encountering Romanians, I spoke German. I could spot them from their poor clothing and tattered luggage. Many were afraid to take complete Bibles because the books were too big to smuggle across the border. But they gladly accepted the smaller Gospels of John.

By the time I finished, I had given away

about fifty Bibles, New Testaments and Gospels of John, and had even found time to return to the platform for more literature.

In the last car, I knocked on the door of a compartment that had milky-white glass. I opened it without waiting for an answer. When the door slid back, I stood face to face with five officials.

During the Ceausescu era, these men ruled the train; it was their territory once the trip began to Romania. Every passenger, no matter his country, is under their authority. They processed papers and inspected luggage. Travelers carefully hid Bibles from official eyes.

Immaculately dressed in uniforms, these guards wore caps with red Communist ribbons and carried large pistols. They were smoking and talking in their seats. I gazed at them and they stared back at me. I could have shut the door immediately and left. Instead, I reached into my pocket and held out a booklet.

"What are you doing here?" one man demanded.

"I'm a Christian from Holland, and I am giving the people in the train each a present."

A muscular official, about forty-five years old, sitting next to the door snapped, "What kind of present?"

I handed him the Gospel of John still in my hand.

His eyes narrowed. "Ahhh. Religion. It is

forbidden on this train." Jumping up, he grabbed me by the shoulder and demanded my passport.

"My passport is at home in Vienna," I answered quickly. "In Vienna, everything is free. You do not have to carry your passport all the time."

He tried to jerk me into the compartment.

"You need to be careful," I advised shakily. "This is a free world." I stepped back into the corridor and quickly left.

He came after me, so I hurried faster. He grabbed the strap of my bag as we ran to the other end of the car. When we reached the door, I turned halfway, ripped the bag away from him and jumped through the opening to the platform.

The guard didn't dare follow, since he had no authority in Austria. But he slid down a window and angrily threw the Gospel of John onto the platform.

I picked up the booklet, and put it back into my bag. Walking alongside the car, I tried to wave to him. Then I returned to my companion, my supply of Bibles exhausted.

Later, I learned that if the glass in the last compartment is milky-white and no one can see through it, don't knock on the door. It's full of officials.

A few days later, I had a brush with another official. It was a warm day and all the doors and windows were open on the train.

As I passed out literature, a woman stood

ABOVE: Gospel through the train window.

LEFT: John B. — A smile is the same in any language.

watching me. After a few moments, she went to the front of the car and spoke to the people behind the compartment with opaque windows. I couldn't hear what she said, but she soon returned with an armed guard. I quickly left.

Even so, the beautiful moments of sharing God's Word with the spiritually hungry travelers completely outweigh the risks. The elderly ladies especially touch me. When I give them Bibles, they kiss me on the cheek with tears in their eyes. They can't say much I can understand, but clasp their hands over their heads to show their gratitude. Then I am reminded that the risks are nothing compared to the rewards of placing God's Word in open hands.

—Jan B.

A Time for Tears

Most "train missionaries" can tell you how they felt the first time they distributed literature. Their experiences are indelibly written on their memories. One pretty blond young woman is no exception. A lovely Christian, she and her husband were members of one of our teams from Belfast, Ireland.

That first day, she wore a long cotton dress and carried a heavy shoulder bag full of literature. She boarded a train waiting to return to Romania and Hungary. She carefully stepped over ruck-sacks, bags, and cases that people were hauling home from the West. Patiently working her way through the crowded compartments, she politely introduced herself to people on both sides of the aisle.

"Are you from Romania?" she asked some of the travelers.

"Are you Hungarian?" she inquired of others.

The passengers smiled and warmed at her friendly voice. By the time she reached the end of the train, she had handed out every piece of literature; her bag was empty. Stepping down onto the platform outside, she stood still and looked back at the crammed cars. Tears began streaming down her cheeks. She felt overwhelmed, thinking of what the Lord had allowed her to witness and experience. I understand how she felt. Her heart was filled with joy at the privilege of giving out the eternal words of life to people so eager to receive.

— David T.

Filling the Emptiness

Over the years I have seen that the Word of God has a particular power to convict men's hearts far more than any other tract or booklet. Most of those reached for Christ on the ships docking in Europe and in trains stopping in Vienna are unbelievers. They have never read the Bible, but they know what it is. Instant recognition fills their eyes when the word

"Biblia" is mentioned. They will go to almost any length to obtain the Word of God to try to fill the emptiness inside their hearts.

This yearning by Eastern Europeans to have their own copy of God's Word is especially shown by another group of travelers — bus passengers. When our team members approach these dear people, they openly express their feelings about the gifts we hand them.

5

"Hands Up for Bibles"

In the center of Vienna lies the Babenbergerstrasse. From early morning until late at night, throngs of tourists from almost every country in the world swarm the street. Many buses — sometimes up to thirty in one morning — stop to unload passengers. Everywhere people are arriving, deciding where to go first, returning with heavy packages, laughing, talking, eating and dozing.

In the middle of this crush of humanity, "bus missionaries" faithfully distribute the Word of God. Using the phrase "please take this" in the language of the contact, they offer Gospels easily recognizable as the "Biblia."

Over the years, the missionaries have developed several valuable methods for sharing Jesus Christ and His Word with these travelers.

First, they identify the nationality of a contact and present him with literature in his own language. Some team members can recognize coaches or buses from the East by the make of the vehicle. A few can distinguish the differences at a thousand yards. One, for example, will spot a bus at the other end of the street and call out to his team mates, "This one's Polish . . . Czech . . . Hungarian." That gives the workers time to prepare the literature for that parking area.

Second, they let the travelers know who they are. Back in their own country, the visitors have never had anyone approach them on the street with something free. At first, many seem reluctant to accept the literature, so the missionaries immediately reassure them that they are not part of a cult or sect, but are true Christian believers. This information is quickly passed by word-of-mouth back onto the bus. In a few seconds, everyone surrounds the missionaries. Sometimes the distributors can't even get the materials out of their rupsacks or shopping trolleys quickly enough to satisfy the demand. The passengers push and shove each other to get sufficiently close to reach the Scriptures.

Third, the teams handle refusals skillfully. If the first few passengers coming off a bus want literature, the others behind them also will accept the gifts. But if one or two refuse, the missionaries quickly back off and let three or four passengers go by. Then the team members resume their distribution, starting and stopping until they get a positive response.

Occasionally the missionaries meet bus drivers who will not let them on his bus or even allow his passengers to open their windows to take the gospel literature. When this happens, one of the missionaries will secretly signal a passenger to get off the coach. Once, a tourist-turned-Bible-smuggler followed the gospel team fifty yards away, where they gathered inconspicuously behind another parked coach. He held out his hands and explained in halting English, "For everyone in the coach, I need . . . I want." He managed to smuggle many gospels aboard his bus.

This scenario happens frequently. Sometimes two or three people step off a bus with bags waiting to be filled with literature. This scene replays two or three times a week. Because of the conditions these Eastern European travelers live under, no one has to teach them how to skirt hostile authorities. It's imbedded in the very nature of their minds. Each of the delegations of new smugglers makes it clear that they have problems getting literature into their countries. But with such hunger for God's Word, these visitors will go to almost any length to receive a Bible or a Gospel. Usually they want Bibles for all their friends, too.

Fourth, the missionaries appeal to parents through their children. These little ones are eager to receive literature; the books — particularly the children's Bibles and Christian comics — are special to them.

The team first shows the literature to their parents for approval, then places the material in their hands. When the adults see the enthusiasm of their children, they request literature for themselves.

Unlike the travelers on trains, coach passengers

seem freer to receive the words of life. On one of my recent journeys to Europe, some of the bus missionaries shared their joys in meeting these tourists. Here in their own words are some of their testimonies:

Hunger in Vienna

Remember the Irish young woman who cried tears of joy on the train platform in Vienna? The following morning, she realized even more how God could use her to touch Eastern Europeans with the gospel, this time as a bus missionary.

We filled our vehicles with our quota of Bibles and New Testaments. (Although we have thousands of Gospels to give away, we have fewer Bibles and New Testaments, so we spread these larger books over as many coaches as we can.) Then we drove to the bus area.

This young woman distributed many Hungarian Bibles. Finally, she had only one left.

Suddenly, she was surrounded by at least half a dozen elderly Hungarian women. They had tanned skins, a few missing teeth and wore black clothes and black head scarves. Each clamored for the last copy of God's Word.

Gazing at their pleading faces, the young woman cried silently, *Who should I give this Bible to? Lord, help me, help me.* She closed her eyes to pray and suddenly felt the Bible being snatched from under her arm. She breathed a sigh of relief, realizing that the impossible decision had been taken out of her hands.

Most of the people on the buses are thrilled to receive Bibles. Many men and women open their wallets, offering to pay for their gifts. Our hearts are torn and moved, and we gently say, "No, this is a gift from God. This is freely given to you. Please accept it."

At times we touch the lives of unbelieving Viennese as well. For example, men or young boys who meet the coaches to sell electrical goods for the local shops. Their skin is dark from working in the sunshine in sandals and shorts and T-shirts. Their job is to pass advertisements to the Easterners.

Even though they do not believe in Jesus, they watch us work and are convinced we are genuine. Sometimes, they even introduce us to people getting off the coaches. Speaking rapidly in their native language, they announce, "Here are believers from England and Ireland! They have Bibles and New Testaments. You should talk to them. They'll give you free gifts."

The interested passengers then approach us, and we point to the bus boys who translate for us. Sometimes the bus boys bring their children along. Since these little ones must sit around for hours waiting for their parents to finish their business, they are delighted to read the children's Scriptures. I recall one special little boy who sat on a bench on the other side of the hedge where the drivers park the buses. He read his comic-strip Bible from cover to cover several times.

Vienna's salesmen and bus boys have willingly helped us many times over the years. What an extraordinary adventure to see unbelievers used by our sovereign God to share His Bread of Life with so many hungry people!

— David T.

Unlikely "Missionary"

God often uses people on the buses to help distribute the literature, but sometimes these unlikely "missionaries" face dangerous situations.

One day, for example, we stopped at the bus stop where we usually find Hungarian visitors. A Czechoslovakian bus was parked there instead. We pulled out our Czech literature and waited for the passengers to return to the empty coach. Two or three people wandered back, so we gave them literature as they boarded.

Then groups of Czechoslovakian travelers began to arrive. We were busy handing out our literature when the bus driver returned. When he realized what we were doing, his face turned red, and he shouted at us angrily. Quickly, he began collecting the literature and giving it back to us. Since we couldn't speak his language, we just smiled sweetly when he dumped the books in our laps.

Meanwhile, as fast as the driver could collect the literature, my friend would redistribute it to the people still getting on the bus. I watched as the driver moved toward the front of the coach with an armful of New Testaments and Gospels of John. When his back was turned, I offered more literature to the passengers through the windows.

One blond, middle-aged woman was especially helpful. It was an amusing sight. Every time the driver turned his back, she took more books and handed them out inside the bus. She was quite pleased with herself, but extremely careful.

In the end, the driver got fed up with giving back the literature, so he put what he had gathered into the locker of the bus. But many of the passengers received a copy of God's Word despite his opposition because of this willing woman. For a few minutes, she became a vital link in our teamwork.

— David N.

Hope for Hungry Hearts

Hungarian buses are especially noticeable. They are instantly recognizable by their colorful signs and decorations which carry the names of the organizations to which they belong — Ibusz, Volan, Cooptourist. They also frequently display the name of the town from which they come. We meet visitors from every corner of Hungary, not only Budapest but also Gyor, Sopron and Szombathely just over the border. The travelers also come from Pecs and Mohacs in the south, from Miskolc in the north and from Debrecen and Nyiregyhaza in the east. No part of the land is missing.

A hunger for God's Word creates unusual situations in our attempts to reach these Easterners for Christ. Many of the coaches, for example, arrive with a tour leader. At first, we were convinced that these guides would be against what we were doing, but often we have been pleasantly surprised. On one occasion, the tour leader handed one of our team members the coach microphone and let him preach.

As he spoke, some of the passengers began to get restless. Suddenly, the tour leader grabbed the microphone and gave the group a good roasting.

"These people have come all the way from England," she scolded loudly. "They try to bring you words about God." She pulled the microphone even closer to her mouth. "You will sit still and listen to them!"

Used to obeying her instructions, the passengers sat quietly and attentively for the rest of the message. I doubt that she was a believer, but God sovereignly used her to touch the others.

One Czech tour leader returned to his coach an hour before his group. He took one of the Gospels and a New Testament we offered. When his group came back to the bus, he would not let them inside, directing them to us instead. Obediently, each passenger walked to us with their hands extended. Only when they had a Gospel clasped in their hands would the tour leader let them board.

Once we distributed literature to a group of Hungarians who had just arrived. They quickly left us and walked up the street to meet another Hungarian bus around the corner. When this second tour group saw the Gospels and learned where the booklets had come from, the people charged in mass. We looked up to see the street full of Hungarians thundering down the sidewalk — straight for us. We were frightened! But all were friendly and had a deep desire to read God's Word.

On another occasion, one of our team — an experienced missionary — found himself on Babenbergerstrasse alone. Everyone else was working in other parts of the city.

Many coaches were arriving so he had no chance of reaching all the visitors. He didn't need to worry. As he gave out literature to one group, he felt his shoulder bag taken from his grasp. Too busy with the heavy press of people, he didn't turn to see what happened.

When he eventually broke free of the crowd, he found his bag empty. A satisfied group of Hungarians were wandering up the street, reading the Gospels. They had simply helped themselves.

Later that summer, another of our workers found himself surrounded by more than two hundred Hungarians and Poles, each seeking a

Gospel. Every one of them was convinced he must get the next booklet or he would be left out.

The crush increased. The worker tried to keep turning so that every corner of the crowd got an equal opportunity to receive literature. But he couldn't turn quickly enough for some. Suddenly, his shirt was torn off by Poles trying to swing him around. Seeing such desire, how can we refuse to use every effort to give these yearning hearts the words of life?

One afternoon, a "dangerous situation" occurred on the Babenbergerstrasse. A group of Hungarians expressed interest in our literature, and a wonderful conversation began. We handed out several Bibles and New Testaments to those who wanted to read more than a Gospel.

When our bags were empty, two elderly women in their sixties suspected we had more Bibles. They grabbed one of the young men handing out literature and bent him against an iron railing, trying to "ring" New Testaments out of him.

I didn't know whether to laugh or cry. Fortunately, I had more New Testaments in my car so we could satisfy everyone. The alarming situation turned into an amusing one.

The excitement of Polish people who learn they can receive a Bible is heartwarming as well. One man who received a Gospel took out his wallet and emptied the entire contents into my hand. He didn't have a single credit card or even a checkbook. He had given me all he had.

Gently, I put the money back into his hand. He was delighted to have a free Gospel. Seeing how seriously he cared about it, I reached into my bag and handed him an entire Bible in his language. He was overwhelmed.

Another Polish man asked me for a Bible. When he had received it, he made me stand beside him while he examined every single page in the book. He couldn't believe that this Bible was written entirely in Polish.

— John R.

Unexpected Opportunities

Sometimes God works in totally unexpected ways.

One day, several of us were driving to the south train station in Vienna. En route, we drove through a park near a big ferris wheel and discovered a Polish bus that had broken down.

Pulling over, we noticed the driver and a few passengers had the back of the bus off and were peering at the engine. Other passengers sat on the grass, while the majority were still in their coach seats looking bored and irritated.

A couple of us began handing Gospels to the passengers sitting on the grass. Quickly, they began flipping through the booklets.

Soon two people from the bus wandered

across the road to our car. When they saw we had Bibles and other materials, they stuck their heads in our boot (automobile trunk). As team members continued to hand books out of the car to our other workers, the curious Poles began asking questions.

Meanwhile, the passengers inside the coach decided this looked like an interesting break, and a few more crossed the road to our car. When they saw the boxes of Bibles, they motioned to their friends still in the coach.

Suddenly forty more streamed from the bus to the back of our car. "Biblia...We would like, too!" they demanded, grabbing at the Bibles still in the boot.

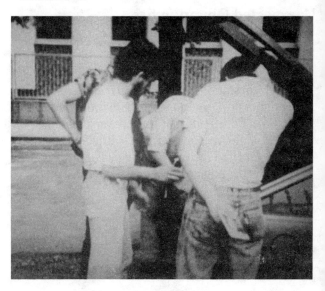

Since we had planned to distribute Polish Bibles and Gospels at the train station, we tried to hold these tourists back. But now men, women and young people were all putting their hands into the boxes. Within minutes, all the literature was gone.

One by one, the passengers sat on the ground to read. As we drove off, they looked up and warmly waved goodbye.

Another time I met a Hungarian coach. I stepped onto the first step, wondering what kind of reception I would find.

The tour guide in charge of the party was using her microphone to explain the sights.

Opening my bag to show her what I had, I asked, "Can we give them out?"

She responded by pulling the microphone to her mouth. "Hands up for Bibles!" she shouted in Hungarian.

I saw hands fly up all over the bus. Everyone wanted the Scriptures.

We walked past her, giving away Bibles, New Testaments and Gospels. How exciting to have our way announced and to find an entire bus full of raised hands!

As we go to reach these people with the gospel, we remember that God has prepared our way. Many times, we find that He has ordered events differently than we expect. And what a joy it is to let Him sovereignly direct and then watch the results!

—Brian L.

The Miracle of Two Hundred Shillings

As a rule, we refuse gifts, particularly money, from those with whom we share the gospel. But one day a group of folk singers from Czechoslovakia insisted that one of our workers accept their generosity. She had no choice but to gracefully take their presents.

The Czechs were touring as a folk festival and were dressed in national costumes. They were so delighted with the Czech Bibles, New Testaments, and children's and evangelistic books she had given them that they began singing folk songs just for her, clapping exuberantly with the music. Then they closed the doors to the bus and would not let her off unless she accepted gifts from them — a bar of chocolate, little ornamental glasses, a record of their songs, and two hundred Austrian shillings.

Returning to our vehicle, she gave me the two hundred shillings to use in our work. I was astounded!

Just that morning, we had had a problem with leaking brake fluid on our car. The dealer quickly fixed the brake. When he heard about our ministry in Austria, he had refused to accept payment. After discussing the price for some time, I had left a gift of two hundred shillings. Now, a few hours later, the Lord had returned our money. What a great God we serve!

— Mike D.

Indescribable Joy

Behind the coach unloading zone is a small park with a few benches and a good stretch of grass. For years, bus missionaries have watched people from many nations sitting in the park reading their new Bibles. Right before their eyes, many hearts begin opening to God. It is truly a wondrous sight.

Quiet now, wind rustling the pages, people intently feed on the Living Word. Youngsters pour over children's leaflets, discovering the story of Jesus for the first time. Old people — born before the Communists came to power and with backgrounds of Orthodox, Reformed or Catholic, but who have never experienced the power of God through His Word — seriously scrutinize the pages. Married couples brought up in atheistic school systems sit on the grass reading together. Many of these people are Communists now disillusioned by Marxism, searching for real truth and hope.

In the few years since this work began, more than 500,000 people have received gospel literature from the "bus missionaries." God knows each one of these hungry hearts and loves them. They are not "The Masses" or "The People." They are precious individuals created by God for His honor and glory.

Wherever East meets West — aboard ships, on trains or in buses — our teams of committed Christian men and women have had the indescribable joy of introducing the Eastern travelers to their first taste of God's Word. But not only have they turned busy harbors, crowded trains and waiting buses into evangelistic centers, even truck stops have become "holy cathedrals" as the gospel teams continue to spread the life-changing Word of God.

6

"Ships" on
the Highways

In July of 1980, Mike, John and Russell set off on a new adventure. Mike had been hooked on distributing Bibles on ocean-going vessels in Bristol, England, so he urged his friends to help him reach a new mission field — "ships" on the highways. The three men packed their bags in a van and sped off to work that morning just like the thousands of other commuters traveling to their jobs. But the new "commuter missionaries" didn't know how to start their work. They just had a burden to share God's Word with the many truckers from the East rolling down the main thoroughfares of Belgium, West Germany, Austria, the Netherlands and Switzerland.

From this simple beginning, an outreach to truckers was born. At first, the commuter missionaries had no strategy for reaching their moving mission field. All they knew was that the drivers presented an opportunity to reach many for Christ. The Lord would have to fill in the details of how to approach these hungry hearts.

Gradually, however, the commuter missionaries began to refine their techniques. They learned in which cities — such as Munich and Vienna — the truck drivers could most easily be contacted.

Some of the missionaries began carrying gifts such as six-ounce bags of candy to pass along to the drivers after offering Scriptures. Around Christmastime, they distributed pairs of woolen gloves to the truckers for their children. Hard-to-find road maps proved particularly effective. When the drivers accepted the gift, the missionaries included a Bible. In this manner, the commercial operators received two kinds of directions — one for the highway on which they are traveling and another to the narrow road that leads to eternal life.

Everywhere they offer God's Word, the commuter missionaries find the same spiritual hunger they have seen on the ships, trains and buses. Several of our workers describe their encounters.

Fertile Soil, Hungry Hearts

That first beautiful July day, Mike, Russell and I set out to reach truckers traveling to the West from Eastern Europe to unload and load cargo. Our first contact was with a Hungarian truck racing down the inside lane of a south German highway at fifty miles an hour. As we pulled alongside him, Mike grabbed a Hungarian Bible from our stock of literature. He hung out his window, hair flapping in the wind, and offered the book to the amazed driver.

"Please take this!" Mike hollered. Our speed whipped his words away. And the Hungarian refused to roll down his window to the "madman" shouting outside his cab.

But we were not discouraged. Near Stuttgart, we saw a long caravan of trucks pulling off the highway into a filling station. They were headed back to the Soviet Union. We pulled in behind them.

Mike and Russell immediately disappeared toward the front line of trucks. I stayed at the back.

The eleven drivers were busy filling up with fuel and checking tires and engines. With officials wandering up and down the line, I wondered whether anyone would take our literature.

But, to our surprise, most of the drivers eagerly accepted our gifts. This became the highlight of our first trip.

We also tried an unusual — and maybe a little reckless — tactic. Whenever we stopped at a red light in traffic, one of us would hurtle out the sliding door of the van. Darting to a vehicle from an East European country, he would thrust literature into the windows of the surprised but grateful drivers. Then he would fly back to the van before the light turned green and the traffic began moving.

We used this method many times over the

next two summers. Sometimes, however, we timed our delivery too close.

Once, while I ran the ten yards back toward our van, the light changed. Mike stepped on the gas.

"John's not in yet!" Russell yelled.

Mike jammed on the brakes which slammed the door shut. I hit the side of the van and bounced off onto the bonnet (hood) of the car in the next lane. A shocked Austrian couple stared at me through their windshield.

After seeing that I wasn't hurt, Mike could hardly contain his laughter. He thought it was hilariously funny until the same thing happened to him another day! Eventually, we abandoned this approach for safer ways.

When we returned from that first trip, the tally of our day's work inspired us to continue. We had distributed more than thirteen hundred pieces of literature to about nine hundred truckers. We realized, too, that these figures didn't reveal the spiritual fruit and growth in the hearts of the individuals we contacted. Only the Lord knew how many of the seeds sown into the fertile soil of hungry hearts would bear fruit. But we looked forward with a sense of excitement to the new opportunities uncovered on our mission to reach "ships" on the highways with the Word of God.

—John R.

"Hunting" for Lorries

My father was a poacher. He always hunted at night. When I was a child, he taught me all he knew about stalking animals. Years later, I used this knowledge to find lorry (truck) drivers.

In hunting, for instance, you find where the animals sleep at night. I knew if I wanted to locate something that was on the move during the day, I had to figure out where it sat at night. So, instead of chasing lorries, I started noting where I had seen them parked. I asked friends who were drivers how far a lorry could travel in one day. Then I worked out likely locations.

Our teams also begin to notice the habits of those we wanted to serve. If lorries of a slightly different shape and size were parked among the others, for instance, then the other drivers would refuse to take our literature. This was strange because some of the truckers had accepted our Bibles before.

Finally, we learned that the odd lorries were military carriers with KGB drivers posing as commercial operators. The Communist government sends these trucks and drivers to check whether lorries from their country can travel easily through various routes. This information would be invaluable in time of war. There are no laws against this deception, but the officials were a problem for us.

We began to notice that the KGB lorries always had two drivers. Unlike the trucker, they wore nice shirts and ties. We also discovered that they were military personnel and that their vehicles were a slightly different shape and size because they were military transports for missiles or tanks.

The special truckers are extremely anti-Christian. The common drivers won't take any Scriptures if the KGB men are near. The officials laugh because they know they have stopped everyone else from getting Bibles. These expeditions are very fruitless.

Sometimes, however, we get good tips about where the lorries park. Late one evening, a police officer phoned our team. "Do you know about the sixty-three Eastern European lorries?" he asked.

We knew the area he described well. But his information came as a surprise. Thrilled with the news, we loaded our car and off we went.

Stopping at the edge of the parking area, we could hardly believe our eyes! Dozens of lorries were parked in a square, tails in. Among them were Hungarian, Yugoslavian and one or two Polish and Romanian trucks. An entire congregation of fish caught in one net!

When we walked into the parking area, the drivers seemed to know we had something for them. Since they are gracious people, they rarely walk up to ask for a gift. Instead, they climbed out of their cabs and stood smiling and expectantly in the bright warm sunshine.

Carrying our heavily laden shoulder bags, we walked along the rows giving out literature, receiving nods, handshakes and quiet greetings. One Hungarian trucker accepted a Bible. So did the man in the next lorry. He spoke in German, asking for a Bible for his wife and two New Testaments for his children. We gladly handed them to him.

When the first driver saw his neighbor get extras, he held up six fingers and mentioned a church situation. We gave him six Hungarian Bibles. He smiled broadly.

A heavy Romanian man with curly brown hair and some of his fingertips missing recognized us and opened the door of his cab. Overcome with emotion, he jumped down and kissed me on both cheeks in his country's fashion. Forgetting himself, he almost kissed my wife Nancy too. When he remembered his manners, he bent ceremoniously low and kissed the back of her hand. Nancy was glad he had restrained himself since he reeked of garlic.

Straightening up, he smiled, "Do you remember me?" We vaguely recalled his face, although all the drivers look somewhat alike in working clothes.

"Do you remember the Bible and the problem with Russia?" he continued excitedly in broken English.

"Yes," we both answered, not quite sure.

"When I got to Russian border, there was a

Russian captain who went through everything. He found the Bible . . . " The Romanian paused. "I wondered what was going to happen to me. The guard told me that this was a very bad thing to have. But he said he was a poor Russian guard because he never made a lot of noise. He said he wouldn't take me to the guard room but would fine me forty rubles instead.

"The officer put the forty rubles in his pocket and gave me back my Bible. I was very happy . . . " He paused again, then continued hesitatingly. "Please give me another one, if you can."

Suddenly, I remembered meeting him a few months earlier. It had been a nervous situation for the drivers we approached. Even in the midst of glasnost, many refused Bibles, not because of Romanian inspections, but because of the Russian searches when the drivers crossed Soviet borders.

Surprised at their fear, I said, "But you're Romanians."

"Yes," the nervous men would answer, crossing their wrists as if handcuffed. "Ah, no, no. Russia, problems. One year Siberia."

We continued to show the group the beautifully illustrated children's Bibles.

The Romanian with the missing fingers said, "Okay. I think I can take one anyway. It's a very nice book."

We promised to pray for him and gave him a Bible.

Now, months later, we saw how God answered our prayers for this courageous man.

We also can't help but notice the habitat of our drivers. Some nationalities from the poorer countries have to sleep in their trucks for several days while waiting for a place on a ship returning home. The inside of a lorry cab in the summertime can reach 90 to 100 degrees. So the drivers suffer the consequences. When we open the doors to these vehicles, a whoosh of pungent air hits us. But when we offer them Bibles, the drivers break out in huge grins.

Our "hunting" for lorries produces wondrous results.

Once, we found a lorry park with one Romanian truck and gave the driver a New Testament. Three days later, we saw a Romanian lorry parked in a different place with the letters RO on the back. When we approached the cab, we met the same trucker. He showed us the bookmark where he had read up to the book of Acts. He had done some intense reading, particularly since he had spent much time delivering his load somewhere across the country.

Most of the drivers have a deep respect for God's Word. I remember a white-headed Romanian trucker doing some mechanical work on his engine. His hands were covered with grease. When we handed him a children's Bible, he held it by the very tip, not wanting to get it dirty. It was something special to him.

This is typical of many drivers. If one is checking his engine or cleaning anything with dirt on it, he still wants his Scripture. But he will hold it so carefully. Many get out a piece of paper or something with which to grab it.

We can guarantee that if we find a lorry park or truck yard where there are ten Eastern trucks, at least two of the drivers will be intently reading their New Testaments before we leave.

Literature is precious to these men. They treat it respectfully. What a joy it is to give them the greatest book of all.

— David N.

Gratitude in Many Languages

The truckers we contact show appreciation for our efforts in many ways.

I recall one rainy day, for example, when we walked into a freight yard where many Bulgarian trucks were parked. We called this place "Red Square." We didn't have official permission to be there, but neither had anyone told us to stay away.

The entrance was flooded, but large truck tires formed a border along the edges, the tops of the tires just above the water. We began to squish our way across the slippery tires with our heavy bags on our shoulders, jumping from one to the next while trying to keep our balance.

Hearing noises, we looked up to see that the

Bulgarians had climbed out of their trucks in the huge yard and were clapping and cheering us on.

I remember another time in particular.

Truck drivers usually park on selected streets in Vienna to rest as they travel from various parts of Eastern Europe with their cargos. We find Romanian trucks parked together, their drivers sleeping in the cabs or sitting nearby.

Often the smell of grilled sausages, bacon and eggs, or other foods fills the air. Not having much money, these truckers have learned to be self-sufficient.

We circulate among them during their get-togethers, saying hello and stopping here and there to chat. We offer them Christian literature and the Scriptures which they eagerly accept. Occasionally, they'll cut a slice of sausage off and present it to us.

I held out a Bible to a driver. He was a big, burly man; I'm only a little chap. He took the book and put it aside with expressions of delight. Wrapping his arms around me in a great big bear hug, he nearly lifted me off my feet.

"Biblia good, Communist no good," he beamed.

I grinned widely, warmed by his enthusiasm.

Some time later, I pulled up behind a Czech truck. As I passed it, I saw three more in front of him. *My word, we've got a real convoy here,* I thought. *I'll have to slow down a bit.*

I let the truck overtake me, then followed the convoy as we traveled up the M-35. *If they continue north, I'll lose them.*

Fortunately, the trucks turned off into London, roaring down a ramp on the left that exited the motorway. They entered an industrial estate with factories on both sides of the road. Pulling in one after another, they parked.

Jumping out into the evening light, I grabbed some literature from the back of my car and hurried over to their cabs. I handed books through the windows saying, "Hello. Gratis . . . free."

I went from cab to cab with Gospels and little booklets, finding eager men ready to receive God's Word. As I drove away, I thought about their reaction. I suppose some people would want to shoot a man who jumped out at them in the night. But these drivers, though amazed, were very friendly and gratefully received the books.

One of the indescribable joys of being a commuter missionary is to see the pleased expressions on the faces of these men as they accept the Bibles. How wonderful to know how much God's Word is treasured by those we serve.

—Brian L.

Rolling Mission Fields of the World

The men and women providing literature to these East European visitors are working on a unique mission field. The ships, trains, buses and trucks from newly liberated Eastern Europe and other Communist lands are the great rolling mission fields that touch many parts of the world. The team members find hearts empty and spiritually hungry for the answer to questions only God can give. By the thousands, the travelers return to their homes to share God's life-changing Word with their families and friends.

As you have seen through these eyewitness accounts, presenting Christ and God's Word to others is an exciting personal adventure. No other experience can give you the deep satisfaction and pure rewards of seeing someone introduced to our loving Savior.

Would you like to know and experience the joy of sharing your faith—whether it be on a ship in port, a train at the station, a bus on a busy street, a truck parked alongside the road or in your own neighborhood? Would you like to taste the thrill of giving others the eternal words of life?

As with any event, preparation is essential if you are going to be successful. I urge you to equip yourself for your journey as you learn from those who have traveled before you. Their failures and successes are their gift to you as you prepare to share Christ and God's Word where you live and work. In the coming pages, I want to suggest some preparations you can make and illustrate a strategy that will enable you to be a more effective witness to the spiritually hungry.

Part 3

Keeping the Cutting Edge Sharp

7

Honing
Your "Ax"

O ne day a young man approached the foreman of a logging crew and asked for a job.

"That depends," the foreman replied. "Let's see you bring down this tree."

The young man stepped forward and skillfully felled the great tree. Impressed, the foreman exclaimed, "You can start Monday!"

Monday, Tuesday, Wednesday and Thursday rolled by, and Thursday afternoon the foreman approached the youth and said, "You can pick up your paycheck on the way out today."

Startled, the young man replied, "I thought you paid on Friday."

"Normally we do," answered the foreman, "but we're letting you go today because you've fallen behind. Our daily felling charts show that you've dropped from first place on Monday to last on Wednesday."

"But I'm a hard worker," the young man objected. "I arrive first, leave last, and even have worked through my coffee breaks!"

Sensing the boy's integrity, the foreman thought for a minute and then asked, "Have you been sharpening your ax?"

The young man replied, "I've been working too hard to take the time."

Has this happened to you? Are you so busy on the front lines for Christ that you have neglected to hone your "ax"? Spiritual preparation through prayer, building up our faith, knowing God's Word and being filled with the Holy Spirit must be constant if we are to remain sharp on the cutting edge of evangelism.

Preparing Through Prayer

Many Christians know about prayer, they believe in its power, they frequently hear sermons on the subject, but it is not a vital part of their lives. Dr. Larry Hughes, Bible professor at Bartlesville Wesleyan College, Bartlesville, Oklahoma, says these Christians suffer from a disease called "miscellaneous." Their prayers and spiritual goals have never been focused. They wander through life a week at a time. As a result, they do not bear spiritual fruit.

But wherever people pray, God works. He presents a clear vision.

There's nothing mysterious about prayer. It is simply talking to God and inviting Him to talk to you. I can think of no greater way to prepare myself for sharing God's Word than through prayer, for it has the power to transform our lives and witness for Christ.

Each of us has a direct line of communication with God at all times. And we are invited to come *confidently* before His throne. "Since we have a great high priest who has gone through the heavens, Jesus the Son of God," Paul writes, "let us . . . then approach the throne of grace with confidence, so that we may receive mercy and find grace to help us in our time of need."[1]

For several practical reasons, prayer is a vital link in your preparation for service. Prayer energizes you for fruitful service, readies hearts to receive Christ, changes people's lives, sets up barriers against Satan, and opens doors of opportunity. Let's look at each of these for a moment:

Energizing for Fruitful Service

Jesus said, "You did not choose me, but I chose you to go and bear fruit — fruit that will last. If you remain in me and my words remain in you, ask whatever you wish, and it will be given you. This is to my Father's glory, that you bear much fruit, showing yourselves to be my disciples."[2] The divine order of fruitbearing is first to talk to God about men and then to talk to men about God. Witnessing, then, is simply harvesting the results of your prayer. Tom V. H. discovered this principle many years ago.

---

[1] Hebrews 4:14-16.
[2] John 15:16,7,8.

Tom became a Christian at the age of thirty-three. After studying in a seminary in Toronto, Canada, he felt God calling him to Holland for a ministry of house-to-house evangelism.

For one year, he visited every home in his new area, and became discouraged with it. The people didn't seem to care. They said, "We have our old age pension, a car in front of the door, and we go on our holidays. What do we need God for?"

Finally one day, Tom stopped on the sidewalk to have an earnest session of prayer with God.

"God, I am sick of this . . . " he began.

Speaking to Tom's heart, the Lord responded, "Unless you are willing to do My will, I can't use you."

So Tom said, "OK, Lord, then give me the grace to continue."

"Suddenly, I became so full of joy that I began to sing," Tom says. "And that was the last day I did that kind of evangelism."

Immediately God opened the way for him to work with the ships, and his years have been filled with fruitful service ever since.

"I'm sixty-four now," Tom says, "and I can play a game of tennis with sixteen-year-old boys as easily as when I was young. Well, almost. God willing, I plan to keep going—maybe as long as the man in Nova Scotia who still visits ships at the age of eighty-four! However long God gives me, one thing is certain: I will never go aboard my floating mission field unless I have spent adequate time with Him in prayer."

As you pray, ask God to renew and quicken your inner person. Ask Him to make you alert and alive — vital, refreshed and always sensitive to the Holy Spirit. Pray for wisdom and guidance and for strength to resist temptation that you will always be fruitful in His service.

Readying Hearts to Receive Christ

For many people, "window shopping" is a pleasurable pastime. They love to roam shopping malls and gaze at the latest fashions behind the display windows or stroll through the aisles of department stores and finger the merchandise. To some Christians, prayer is like window shopping — they spend much time looking but never buy anything. Prayer is more than browsing through God's storehouse of blessings. It involves winning souls through intercession.

Jesus is our great example. The apostle Paul writes, "He is able to save completely those who come to God through him, because he always lives to intercede for them."[3]

Intercession is a silent ministry which seldom gets noticed. But much of our success in evangelism can be traced back to the moments we spend in prayer. Walter B. gives testimony to this fact as he ministers to Bulgarian seamen in an English harbor:

"Late one night in the darkness, I drove slowly along the quayside praying, 'Lord, bring men to me.'

---

[3] Hebrews 7:25.

Two Bulgarians suddenly appeared at my car window. I whispered that I had Bibles. At the boot of my car they took nine Bibles and hid them away before they ascended the gangway to their ship. Within minutes, another man appeared and grabbed a Bible. After hiding it down his trousers, he too disappeared.

"My prayer of thanks to God was interrupted as a huge weather-beaten figure using sign language urged me to wait. Shortly afterwards he was joined by a smaller man. Getting into my car, we sped homewards. These men came with me five times to church in secret.

"When that ship eventually sailed, I thanked God for these men and rejoiced that on board were twenty-three Bibles and many Scripture portions.

"Many Poles have come to church with me. On one occasion, six from one ship came back to my home, and around the fireside, we chatted about Calvary and the way of salvation. The next day there was a knock on my door, and there stood four of them. They had walked all the way from their ship. Their one purpose was to find Christ.

"Over coffee, my wife and I and my friend Mervyn explained to them again the steps to repentance. Their spiritual eyes were opened, and they knelt with us to pray. Rising, we shook hands as brothers in Christ. They sailed the next day with new life inside them."

Changing People's Lives

The apostle Paul said, "I pray for you constantly." No wonder the Christians whom he helped to disciple showed such a revolutionary quality in their lives. Genuine, biblically based prayer so changes those who pray that God can reveal His will to them and release His great power through them to change the course of people and nations. The faithful prayers of believing Christians have proven this over and over again.

I recall a time of simple, honest prayer before God which changed my life. It took place while I was still on Grand Cayman. I was in my early twenties, a school teacher, and had a deep yearning to do something for God.

The island was only three miles wide and seventeen miles long. Beside one stretch of the road that parallels the ocean lay an old foundation for a house that had long ago crumbled. I chose that spot to pray one day because I would be out of view from passing traffic. The foundation was bordered with trees and tropical plants. I stood in the center of this nature sanctuary. Little did I realize how seriously God would take my prayer.

"God, here I am," I began. "You know me. What can You do with me? I would really like to make a difference in the world for You, but there's not really much here to offer You. I don't know how much I'm worth, but I have a tremendous amount of desire to serve You. I pray that in spite of who I am, You will give me a chance to do great things for You."

I was holding my big Thompson Chain reference Bible. Suddenly, I laid the Bible on the ground and stood on it. "Lord, regardless of the ups and downs of my life, no matter what direction You want me to take, I want to stand on this," I wept. "This is my authority for what I can do in Your kingdom."

From that moment, I felt a deeper sense of commitment to Christ and the assurance of His guidance.

The Bible commands us to "pray without ceasing" because prayer is the basis of spiritual power. Those of us who are on the front lines of evangelism understand this well. Prayer often brings dramatic change in the lives of those who strongly oppose the gospel. A Canadian missionary, for example, knelt as his Chinese Communist interrogator mockingly commanded him to pray and demonstrate that God answers prayer. The missionary prayed that God would make it apparent that He does answer prayer, even if it meant that the brash interrogator would lose his sight.

Immediately the man was blinded, just as Elymas was in Acts 13. As a result, seven other prisoners and the interrogator received Christ. Eventually the converted interrogator died as a Christian martyr at the hands of his former comrades.

Setting Up Barriers Against Satan

As Christians we are constantly at war with three formidable forces — the world, the flesh and the devil.

No one who loves the things of this world more than God has ever been used of Him in any significant way. If Satan can't stop us in any other way, he will work through the love of the world to divert us from God's plan for our lives.

We will have conflict in our flesh for as long as we live. Perhaps scores of times every day — at home, while working or shopping or driving our car — we face temptations to compromise our Christian convictions. No matter how spiritually mature we are, we will experience temptation. At no time in this life will we ever be free from it.[4]

Conflict with Satan is inevitable — especially if we are invading his territory with the light of the gospel. We must be prepared for war, ever alert to his cunning and subtle attempts to defeat and destroy us.[5]

In each of these areas — the world, the flesh and the devil — prayer is a vital weapon. The apostle Paul says, "The weapons we fight with are not the weapons of the world. On the contrary, they have divine power to demolish strongholds."[6] Through prayer, you have the power to pull down the "strongholds" which prevent you from accomplishing your task. Talking to God will keep you in touch with Him and enable you to appropriate His power in your life. Only in this way may you live victoriously and be an effective witness for Christ.

---

[4] Galatians 5:17.
[5] 1 Peter 5:8,9.
[6] 2 Corinthians 10:4.

Opening Doors of Opportunity

Have you ever attempted to do something for the Lord only to have the door of opportunity slam shut in your face? It happens to all of us.

Prayer, however, is God's key for unlocking closed doors. "This is one of the greatest lessons I've learned as I carry out my missions," Tom V. H. says.

On one occasion the Lord directed him to visit a Russian ship anchored in a specific harbor in his port mission field. It was the only vessel in that harbor, and the gangway had not been lowered.

"Lord, You sent me to this ship," he prayed earnestly as he walked up to it. "Now, please let the gangway come down."

Suddenly, from nowhere, a man appeared. Tom shouted his request to come aboard, and the man let down the gangway then disappeared.

As Tom climbed on board, the crew mistook him for the harbor pilot. This gave him the advantage he needed. Tom gave away all the Bibles he had and was back on the wharf within five minutes.

Coincidence? I don't think so. Prayer is the essential key to opportunity.

Just south of Vienna lies a refugee camp which over the years has taken in thousands of emigres from many countries, including Albania. The evacuees are housed in a run-down old mansion, which at one time must have been a magnificent building with big rooms and corridors. Men and women are segregated, with fifty or more people crammed into each room and sleeping in bunks stacked virtually to the ceiling. With railings all around the camp and a police check-point, you can't just come and go.

Outsiders are not allowed to enter without a special pass, but this does not keep Jan B. and his team from sharing the gospel with these emigrants. One hot July morning they loaded their gray Opel station wagon with Russian, Bulgarian, Albanian and Romanian Bibles, cassette recordings of Christian music and other literature, and headed for the camp. They parked near the tall, iron front gate, then caught the attention of a thin man walking behind it.

Jan asked him in German what his nationality was. He said Romanian. Jan reached through the bars and gave him a Romanian Bible and a cassette of Christian music. The man looked stunned.

"You must call all of the Romanians you know in the camp. Bring them to the gate," Jan told him. "Tell them I have a present for them."

Workers of the Wurmbrand missions in Vienna spending an evening "honing their axes."

The man left, and in five or six minutes, twenty people arrived. All were poorly dressed and had been in the West for less than a week. The group approached cautiously. Conferring in whispers for a moment, they appointed a boy to walk up to the gate. As he approached, Jan and his team took the Bibles and cassettes out of the boxes and held them in the air.

"Look! We have gifts for you," they said.

The boy translated for them, and as soon as his friends heard the word 'Biblia,' they rushed in mass to the gate and stretched their arms through the bars trying to grab a Bible.

With cries of "Give me Biblia" in their ears, the team busily unpacked the boxes on the pavement. Jan's daughter Heleen, her boyfriend, and another Christian brother shoved the contents through the bars. The people stood in rows of two or three, some leaning up over others against the walls. One woman climbed back through the group and kissed her Bible, tears pouring down her cheeks. Others stood around in a circle, lovingly caressing the Bibles.

Two days later as the team was pulling up to the entrance, they saw a new group. All were standing neatly on the outside of the gate with the same translator boy. The refugees had completed their registration with the government and were allowed to go outside and shop.

"When they recognized my Dutch license plate," Jan recalls, "they circled the car as I turned off the motor. Most happily received a Bible and music cassettes. A few men held back. They were Albanians.

Heleen smiled and handed them a New Testament in Albanian. They were delighted. All 2,169 churches in their Communist country had been destroyed or closed, yet their hearts always remained open."

It was difficult if not impossible to enter this refugee camp due to the many restrictions while they were being processed. But Jan and his team had prayed that morning that God would show them a way to reach them. "Lord," Jan prayed, "You are the mighty one; You can open these doors."

After their morning prayer time, Jan walked up to the police officer standing in the little guard house. "He motioned me inside where I sat down beside him. I showed him the Bibles, and he allowed my co-workers to drive the car inside the camp.

"Mathilde stayed with the car and gave out literature to those who passed, while the rest of us went inside the rooms of the compound."

Amid the smells of closely confined people and the chaos of playing, running children, they prayed and wept with the people, giving them the Scriptures and discussing their problems.

"How the people miss this love!" Jan says. "It helps them to speak of their suffering, then we can share in their joys of receiving the gospel."

Today the window to Albania is cracking open. Will we learn from the Christians there as we rush in to help them? Will dozens of Western pastors, never having really suffered one day for Christ, hurry in to win fame and "teach" them? How many pastors will first spend years or months or even one day to "listen" to these Christians?

The Basic Imperative

Early in my ministry I discovered that prayer is an indispensable part of preparation. I recall one occasion while staying with an Amish family on their Indiana farm. I had been invited to speak in their church and was in prayer while pacing up and down between the rows of their harvested cornfield.

"I want to see my spirit develop and become stronger," I prayed. "I want the temptations of the flesh to be brought under the control of the mind of Christ. I feel I can accomplish so much more in those countries that are desperately hungry for You. When the Christians in America see a real need, they respond. Help me to know how to communicate that need."

Point by point I laid out what I wanted God to do in my life and ministry. Some may call this arrogant. But I believe He delights in hearing us ask boldly for spiritual things.

I can think of no greater way to win the heart of God than to be humbly bold before Him. I encourage you to be totally honest with the Lord in your prayers. Completely yield yourself to His will and spend time with Him in loving, intimate conversation every day. God will indeed do great things through you.

Prayer is not only the key to opportunity, it is the indispensable condition of power. And along with building your faith through the Word of God, it is the basic imperative of your preparation for spiritual battle.

8

Where No Road Exists

When Dr. David Livingstone was working in Africa, a group of friends wrote to him, "We would like to send other men to you. Have you found a good road into your area yet?"

According to a member of his family, Dr. Livingstone sent this message in reply: "If you have men who will come only if they know there is a good road, I don't want them. I want men who will come if there is no road at all."

Many Christians are afraid to go where no road exists. Having been taught to trust the religious structure around them rather than Christ, they become insulated and lose touch with the world. Dr. Oswald Smith's church in Toronto has supported and sent hundreds of missionaries around the world. Dr. Smith has a shockingly realistic interpretation of Jesus feeding the five thousand which illustrates our upside-down religious emphasis:

Do you remember when the Lord Jesus

Christ fed the five thousand? Do you recall how He had them sit down, row upon row, on the green grass? Then do you remember how He took the loaves and fishes and blessed them and then broke them and gave them to His disciples? And do you remember how the disciples started at one end of the front row and went right along that front row giving everyone a helping? Then do you recall how they turned right around and started back along that front row again, asking everyone to take a second helping? Do you remember?

No! — a thousand times — no! Had they done that, those in the back rows would have been rising up and protesting most vigorously. "Here," they would have been saying, "Come back here. Give us a helping. We have not had any yet. We are starving; it isn't right; it isn't fair. Why should those people in the front rows have a second helping before we have had a first?"

And they would have been right. We talk about the second blessing. They haven't had the first blessing yet. We talk about the second coming of Christ. They haven't heard about the first coming yet. It just isn't fair. *"Why should anyone hear the Gospel twice before everyone has heard it once?"* You know as well as I do, that not one individual in that entire company of five thousand men, besides women and children, got a second helping until everyone had had a first helping.[1]

David Livingstone and other great missionaries

---

[1] Oswald J. Smith, *The Challenge of Missions* (Bromley, England: Lakeland STL Books, 1959), p. 36.

have understood this concept. Their vision was for the world. They went to feed the back rows.

Christ's command to "go into all the world" was given to people — to me and to you. We cannot hide behind the name of our particular church and its accomplishments. It is our task to find new locations where roads do not exist and then to build them. But we cannot do this effectively without knowing God's Word.

Why Has the Bible Been a Forbidden Book?

The work of distributing Bibles among seamen, tourists and truckers from Communist lands has opened dramatically since glasnost began its thaw in East-West relations. Although fear and suspicion still linger in the minds of many of our Eastern visitors, they are wondering, "Why has the Bible been a forbidden book?"

Bibles decorate the coffee tables, book shelves and bed stands of many Western homes, rarely leaving those pedestals except for a token visit to church on Sunday morning.

Yet the eternal future of every person we meet may very well rest in our own daily study of the Bible because the Scripture reveals God's heart for the world and energizes us for service. In sharing the gospel, have you ever felt confused and alone — unsure of yourself or of which way to turn in a situation? The Scripture is not only for practical everyday living, but it inspires and energizes us to declare Christ's message effectively.

God's Word develops our faith. The apostle Paul writes, "Faith comes from hearing the message, and the message is heard through the word of Christ ..."[2] Every time you and I read and study God's Word, we are building up our faith which, like a muscle, grows with exercise.

Although Jesus spoke of faith the size of a mustard seed, that doesn't mean He wants us to think small. Someone has said, "Small plans do not inflame the minds of men." How big is your faith? When you think of the Lord's command to reach the world, can you ask Him for too much in accomplishing your mission?

Faith produces miracles when we pray expectantly. Jesus promises, "If you believe, you will receive whatever you ask for in prayer."[3] But your faith must be anchored to God's Word, for it is the only sure word of truth, and you can stake your life on its promises.

God's Word defends our call. When you are launching into a new area of ministry for Christ, you undoubtedly will come under attack. Not necessarily by Satan. Indeed, he is a relentless foe. But other Christians or Christian groups may object to your approach.

Dropping literature from aircraft, for example. Although Trans World Missions and other organiza-

---

[2] Romans 10:17.
[3] Matthew 21:22.

tions have done this over Mexico and other countries for years, this highly unorthodox method of evangelism draws fire from some sectors of the Christian community. Some have even wondered if my imprisonment for dropping Gospels and other Christian literature over Cuba may have been just.

My seven years of periodic literature drops over and around Cuba were no James Bond flash-in-the-pan activity. It was a concerted effort to penetrate the island of fear with the gospel of love.

Sometimes we must resort to the unorthodox to reach the world for Christ. As long as what we do does not violate the principles of God's Word, we have a defense in our Lord's command to go. We must base our endeavors on the Great Commission and the tenets of Christ's teachings. We dare not launch out for the Lord depending on the praise of others. Perhaps most of the top Christian ministries in the world today would never have been started — or would not have grown as rapidly — had their founders waited for other Christians to approve.

The Scripture lays out clean, honest principles. By letting them guide you, God will open opportunities for ministry you never thought possible. Often He prepares a parallel track for your life. I studied to be an English teacher. In the meantime, God was also getting me ready to spread His Word by sea and by air. Perhaps you are a student, a homemaker, grocery clerk, secretary, businessman, doctor or other professional person. Ask God to show you His other footprint for your life. How can you best serve Him? Wherever He calls, His Word will defend.

God's Word gives answers to tough questions. Everywhere you turn people are confused about life. They are groping for answers to its perplexing questions. They want to know what the Bible has to say about their world, how they can survive. Frequently these issues must be satisfied before people will accept the gospel. If you know the Scripture, you will be able to respond with confidence as this story illustrates:

One very warm day, Billy J. was stepping up the plank of a Bulgarian oil tanker docked in Dublin. Suddenly, he was stopped by a KGB agent on the ship and escorted to the captain's office. Sitting behind his desk, the short, stern-looking officer had pulled his shirt sleeves back trying to look important.

With all the courage Billy J. could muster, he tried to sound cheerful. "Welcome to Dublin."

"What is your business on my ship?" the captain shot back.

Billy handed him a Bible in Russian. "I'm from The Seaman's Friend Mission. I'm bringing Bibles free for you and for all the members on your ship."

Curious, the captain reached for the Bible and opened it. Suddenly, his face began to redden. "You have some cheek coming on board my ship and telling me about the God in this book!" he sputtered. Pushing his chair back and standing, he blurted angrily, "Look at your own country; look at Ireland: They're killing one another, and they call themselves *Christians!* Pick up any paper and you see nothing but wars and troubles; look at the children that are sick; look at the disease in the world and you tell me about the God in *that* book!"

Billy interrupted the officer's tirade. "Now, Captain, calm down. Let me show you something." Turning to Mark 13, he read from verses 7 and 8:

> When you hear of wars and rumors of wars, do not be alarmed. Such things must happen, but the end is still to come. Nation will rise against nation, and kingdom against kingdom. There will be earthquakes in various places, and famines . . .

Not waiting for the captain's response, Billy explained, "See, the things you mentioned are in this book. The Bible was written 2,000 years ago, and yet it is relevant for today."

Grasping the Bible, the amazed captain mused, "I never knew this was a good book. I want to keep this one."

After this Billy was able to pass out more Bibles on that ship. God had made a new road for the Russian sailors.

God earlier had made a new road for Billy, too. Once a heavy drinker, Billy had forsaken friends and family and was living in an abandoned railway car in the London area. He returned one day to the tracks to find that a locomotive had carried his "home" away, taking all his belongings. Desperate, Billy called Bob Irvine of the London City Mission. Bob led Billy to Jesus Christ.

Unknown to many outside of Ireland, there are

Irish Christians — the true believers — north and south who have Christ's mercy and grace in their hearts, not hatred and death. If the others on that beautiful island followed the teachings of Jesus like Billy instead of merely being outwardly religious, death would be overwhelmed by new life.

Building Up Your Faith

Billy's spiritual growth and strength came through consistent study and application of God's Word in his life. Martin Luther once said that he studied his Bible in the same way he gathered apples. First, he shook the whole tree, that the ripest might fall; then he shook each limb, and when he had shaken each limb, he shook each branch, and after each branch, every twig; and then he looked under every leaf.

This great reformer admonishes us to search the Bible as a whole — thus shaking the whole tree — reading it rapidly as we would any other book. Next, he says, shake every limb — study book after book. Then shake every branch, giving attention to the chapters when they do not break the sense. Now shake each twig by a careful study of the paragraphs and sentences. Finally peer under each leaf by searching the meaning of the words.

Taking a few minutes each day to read a chapter is a good way to start. But we should also block out extended periods of time to explore God's Word and reflect on what He is saying to us. This is absolutely essential to our preparation for sharing the gospel.

Here are some well-known steps you can take in your preparation:

Begin your study with prayer. Ask the Holy Spirit to make the sacred truths of Scripture real to you. Ask Him to help you understand the meaning of each passage, then apply those truths to your life.

Study the Word with a thirst for truth. Jesus says, "Blessed are those who hunger and thirst for righteousness. If you hold to my teaching, you are really my disciples. Then you will know the truth, and the truth will set you free."[4]

Study with a humble heart. "The sacrifices of God are a broken spirit," the psalmist writes. "A broken and contrite heart, O God, you will not despise."[5] Approaching your study of the Scripture in this manner will enable the Holy Spirit to quicken within you the cleansing power of His Word.

Another way to build up your faith is to associate with living saints. My father never went to church. Nor did he have much to do with me as a child. As a result, I grew up with a big gap in my life. But in the process, I discovered strength in identifying with strong Christians. The faith of my mom and other believers I grew up with pulled me through some rough times. I would go on trips with them. I would ask them questions. I would feed on their answers. Somehow being around Christians who were highly

---

[4] Matthew 5:6; John 8:31,32.
[5] Psalm 51:17.

dedicated and motivated for the kingdom rubbed off on me, and I gained the courage to go on.

In later years, I found inspiration in such heroes of the faith as Corrie ten Boom and Richard Wurmbrand. Their faith under torture helped me tremendously during my own times of suffering while imprisoned in Cuba. Pastor Wurmbrand's influence on my life is one of the reasons I am associated with *Christian Missions to the Communist World* today.

Reading books about missionaries and martyrs also will build up your faith. My mother read to me *Fox's Book of Martyrs* before I was twelve years old. While I was a teacher on Grand Cayman and after I returned to the United States, I studied the plight of Christians in oppressed countries. Believers from Romania, Bulgaria and Russia stayed in my home. All of them former prisoners for their faith and witness — Vasile Rascol, David Klassen and others — were living stories, not history. The great sacrifices of the early Christians and the unwavering commitment of these modern martyrs to our Savior permeated my character and broadened my own depth of dedication.

The stories of today's Christian heroes are in a sense part of the Bible. I've always been told that the Book of Acts has never been finished. Christian believers have long journeyed the rugged trails of tragedy and traveled the wide boulevards of triumph. And with each step, they have fired new acts of courage to inspire us all.

As a prisoner in Cuba, I didn't experience over-whelming grief over my confinement. Rather, I looked at my miseries as an extension of the sufferings of others. Perhaps the great reason for this — other than my faith in Christ that was founded on His Word — was that I had already suffered vicariously through the powerful stories and personal examples of other Christians under fire. I saw myself as one of them. They gave me courage when I needed it most.

Another way to build up your faith is to go on a weekend or vacation "vision trip." I hitchhiked down to Mexico alone once when I was just nineteen to visit some missionaries and learn how they worked. I wouldn't advise hitchhiking for today, of course. But that trip helped give me a vision for the world. I've met many people whose lives have been changed or who have heard the call of God for special service because they went to a third-world nation just for a week.

Catherine Marshall once wrote a one-sentence comment about faith: "Faith is not even worthy of the name until it erupts into action." Faith is never passive. It demands a response. It asks for a mission. It demonstrates the indwelling presence and power of the Holy Spirit.

Energizing Your Faith

Let me take you back for a moment to the dusty trails of the Palestine that Jesus knew. For more than three years, twelve men walked beside Him almost daily; they heard Him teach, saw Him heal, and watched Him perform miracles. But they were filled with jealousy, frustration, fear and unbelief. And just

The political officer on this large Cuban ship made us leave.

But we passed much literature to the crew while he was throwing us off.

when our Lord was faced with His darkest hour of crisis, they deserted Him.

Something happened to them on the Day of Pentecost, however. When they were filled with the Holy Spirit, their lives changed. Once unbelieving, powerless and fruitless, they became bold with faith, energized with power and abundant with spiritual fruit. And from the "Upper Room," they went forth to evangelize a lost world undaunted by persecution and martyrdom.

Jesus said, "This is to my Father's glory, that you bear much fruit, showing yourselves to be my disciples."[6] The only way you and I can produce fruit is through the power of the Holy Spirit. By inviting Christ to live His resurrection life in and through us by His Spirit, we will bear spiritual fruit as naturally as a healthy vine brings forth its abundance.[7]

Now . . . as wars are fought with detailed plans of action, we too must prepare for a successful mission. We are in a spiritual battle which requires a different kind of strategy. We need a new way of thinking.

---

[6] John 15:8.
[7] John 15:1-8.

9

Planning a Successful Mission

Reading the newspaper one Monday morning, I learned that a large troupe of Czechoslovakian dancers and musicians would be at the community center in our Oklahoma town that Friday evening for a concert.

I scanned the article excitedly wondering how I could find a way to reach these foreign visitors. Picking up the telephone, I quickly dialed Ruth Yoder at our Mission office.

"Ruth, is there any way we can get Czech Bibles or Bible portions sent to me by Friday?"

She was eager to help. "I'll have them sent Express Mail today."

Ruth called one of our many contacts, and two days later I had sixty booklets of Scripture in the Czech language. Sixty books, sixty Czechs: how would God put them together?

That week I had two speaking engagements — the singles group of my church and the chapel service of Bartlesville Wesleyan College. At both events I challenged my audiences about reaching the Czechs. Many wanted to help.

I could see God's hand working. I had the literature and the volunteers. All that remained was a strategy.

Troupe Surveillance

We all met in the basement of my home. My wife Ofelia treated us to brownies and ice cream as we prayed and planned. I'm sure that when baby Moses' basket touched the water, his mother didn't want to make a "big splash" in hiding her son from Pharaoh. Similarly, God's people can work quietly and calmly in special gospel work. We decided that our best approach would be to attend the concert and simply blend in.

We began to develop our strategy, determining to leave no place uncovered where the troupe would be. Doors, exits, hallways, the orchestra pit, dressing rooms, buses, hotels—each area had to be manned. But how would we accomplish this task? Surveillance of the concert hall and hotel where the troupe would be staying, we concluded, had to be one of our first duties.

On Friday I dressed in my best suit and drove to the community center concert hall for a pre-concert reception open to the public. Phyllis, a friend in the church choir, went to the hotel and sat in the lobby to observe and watch for opportunities while the others carried out their various assignments.

The situation at the community center looked tight. There were cameras in the hallways. The audience would not be mixing with the musicians or dancers, not before or after the concert. Security guards would be stationed at the hallways leading to the dressing rooms.

When Phyllis joined me, she was bubbling with excitement. She had given some literature to a Czech who was walking from the hotel to a van and had learned that the entertainers were in their dressing rooms in the back of the concert hall.

At an appropriate time, I walked out of the center and around to the rear of the building. The outside entrance was open. Quietly entering back stage, I approached three ladies dressed in elegant costumes and putting on the last touches of their makeup in front of mirrors. Here was my chance.

I tried the only Czech sentence I had learned that week from Bob Brchan, *Toje dar protebe* — "This is a gift for you." Smiling, I held the pink Scripture booklets out to them. The ladies took them, curious that someone would give them literature in their own language. I turned around and saw an elderly woman seated on a stool mending costumes. I gave her a booklet. She smiled faintly and quickly slipped it under the costume on her lap.

Returning to the concert hall, I met Randy, Lisa and Jim, and we placed Scriptures on the orchestra chairs or on top of the musical instruments. Would these people be open to the gospel? Would they be afraid, too sophisticated, indifferent? Would they get angry and protest?

We were sitting spaced apart on the first row just in front of the orchestra pit when the musicians arrived and began preparing. Each of us prayed silently as we studied their reactions to the gospel literature.

The musician who sat in front of me, a silver-haired man with a moustache who played the bass viol, unceremoniously removed the Scripture portion from his instrument and placed it on his chair. Soon the music began. Drums, flutes, violins, clarinets, and a piano-like instrument played by a young woman with sticks harmonized beautifully. The folk dancers were graceful and enthusiastic in their wonderfully artistic performance.

But we were engaged in a far more beautiful art — the art of spiritual warfare, a battle involving angels and heavenly places.

I prayed intensely for the violist while visualizing myself before the door of heaven pounding on it, pleading with God for this man, claiming that the blood which Jesus shed would be applied to him also. Our eyes were at the same level as he stood in the orchestra pit. From time to time, he would scan the audience nervously, and our eyes would meet. Once I held up the pink book of Scripture as I clapped, and he saw it.

At intermission the orchestra players picked up their instruments and left. All of the little booklets were gone, except for one. The bass player for whom

I had been praying had left his on the chair. Was he afraid? Would he get it later?

Several of us hurried to the back stage door and strode boldly into the dressing room area. I stepped up to the male dancers who were changing clothes and began handing out the booklets and dropping them into open clothing chests or placing them on hats. Within a few moments, we distributed the literature to everyone back stage and to some waiting outside.

After the concert, the bass viol player meticulously folded his music as the other musicians began filing out. Once alone, he bent down and covered the little book with his large hand, slid it inside his shirt, then walked up the steps to go back stage.

We continued distributing the rest of the litera- ture amazed by the warmth of the troupe's reception to our gifts. We left the parking lot that night thanking God for breaking down the walls of our narrow vision and for allowing us to be "foreign mission" workers in the heartland of America.

Czechoslovakia still needs us. They want our Bread. We talk of Eastern Europe now being free. But Michael Novak reports:

> In Czechoslovakia, public resentment is building up because six months after the revolu- tion, the hated secret police are still on the payroll and (some think) up to the same old work. Those who suffered under their whip find this in- tolerable. It is known that the secret police have a list of 150,000 paid informers and perhaps enough

other material to destroy careers for many years to come.[1]

If we are to reach the people from these countries, we must continue to plan.

Preparing for Your Mission

Planning is not always easy. Many of the unusual techniques used by these Christian workers were born out of frustration. Even so, to be effective it is good to be aware of a few principles.

Be flexible. Any successful work requires flexibility. Often we must adapt to situations where advance preparation is impossible or where the best of plans go wrong. In developing our approach for reaching the dance troupe, no amount of planning could have prepared us for the unpredictable moments. Most Christian workers know the value of adapting to unforeseen circumstances.

Alan C. recalls an incident in a small port town in the northern islands of Scotland. Christians burdened for the thousands of foreigners visiting their port had erected a banner in the market square which read in Russian, "Christ Is Risen!" Some dark-skinned men wearing working overalls who had seen the banner came into the local Christian mission. In their hands were invitation cards they had received on the street for coffee at the mission.

Fascinated by the literature table, they rummaged through the Bibles until they found one in their

---

[1] *Forbes*, June 11, 1990.

own language. Carefully opening them, they talked together for a moment then walked over to the table where Alan was sitting.

He had spread a map on the table, and the seamen pointed out where they lived: Azerbaijan, a Soviet state in the south above Iran. They asked many questions, and with the help of an interpreter, Alan began to show them some verses in the Gospel of John in his specially marked Russian Bible. But the Azerbajaniis were not happy with that. They wanted to read the passages in their own Bibles, following Alan closely and using their fingers at times to underline the words.

"We went through Christian booklets which included diagrams and illustrations," Alan says. "I could more easily use these without an interpreter. Sometimes though, I would be stuck when pointing to an illustration. I would pause, not knowing what to do. Once one of the Azerbajaniis smiled and delightedly gave me the Russian word."

Another had a question. "Who is Solomon? Is he in the Bible?" Alan explained about the Old and New Testaments, about Solomon, and invited one of the men to read selected passages while the other listened.

It's hard to describe the essence of these holy moments, but one thing is certain: Such times cannot be planned.

Graham and Robyn S. in Brisbane, Australia, for example, were placing gift-wrapped Russian Bibles in the hotel rooms of the Bolshoi Ballet. At one room a large, bearded Russian dressed in his bathrobe opened his door just as Robyn was sliding a Bible under it. He was sick and could not perform. Robyn quickly straightened up, mumbled a word of greeting, and hurried away. The next day they learned that the one hundred Bibles they had left were all eagerly taken by the Russians.

Once Graham and Robyn waited in a hotel lobby in Queensland for a Russian trade delegation. The elevator doors opened and the Russians walked out with a man dressed as an Orthodox priest. Entering in a discussion with them, the two Australians offered them Russian Bibles. The "priest" protested more than the others. At first he would not take them, saying that there are plenty of Bibles in the Soviet Union. Finally, the group accepted the "love gifts." Later the priest was exposed in a magazine as a KGB agent stationed in Egypt.

A yearl later Grham and Robyn, supplied by Merv Knight, took Bibles to another hotel. They were learning not to be surprised by unexpected situations. One big muscular man with the Soviet delegation grabbed Robyn and locked her into a tremendous hug.

"You beautiful Australian woman," he gushed, "I want to take your picture to remember the beautiful Australian woman who gave me this Bible. I will put your picture on the wall in my room."

Robyn managed to pull herself out of his grasp and escape his camera.

Focus on a clear objective. No matter how flexible, you must have a clear objective when preparing for an outreach. Keeping this goal firmly in mind will enable you to persevere when circumstances are not ideal or when opposition arises.

The apostle Paul was a master at this. At the Areopagus in Athens he encountered a group of Epicurean and Stoic philosophers who challenged his presentation of the gospel. Paul called their attention to one of the Greek altars.

"Men of Athens!" he exclaimed. "I see that in every way you are very religious. For as I walked around and observed your objects of worship, I even found an altar with this inscription: TO THE UN-KNOWN GOD. Now what you worship as something unknown I am going to proclaim to you."[2]

Can you hear the determination in Paul's voice? His one objective was "to preach to the Gentiles the unsearchable riches of Christ."[3] His single focus was never in doubt. To the Corinthians he said, "When I came to you, brothers, I did not come with eloquence or superior wisdom as I proclaimed to you the testimony about God. For I resolved to know nothing while I was with you except Jesus Christ and him crucified."[4]

Such dedication has compelled Mike D. and his co-workers in their efforts to reach the performers of the Russian state circus.

Every year the circus comes to Durham Downs, a vast expanse of land in England. Some time ago

---

[2] See Acts 17:16-23.
[3] Ephesians 3:8.
[4] 1 Corinthians 2:1,2.

Mike D. and his friends decided to circulate among the performers and distribute Gospel portions. But first they visited the Downs for several days to study the situation.

"The performers didn't stay at the site," Mike recalls. "We knew their pattern. Usually, they stayed in a hotel and came to the circus grounds by bus. But this time we didn't know where the hotel was. We took some of the girls who had done European literature work with us and waited in the Downs area."

Finally a coach full of performers arrived, and the team ran up to give Scriptures to all who wanted them. One of the grateful Russians gave Mike an official circus lapel badge.

About six in the evening the following day, Mike and his workers decided to "join the circus." They walked between some railings, then through the red and blue canvas flaps into the big tent where they found the Russians seated at long tables eating.

The actors were not only hungry for cabbage and dry brown bread, but they hungrily reached out for Christian literature as well. They were especially responsive when they saw that the literature was in their own language.

Suddenly Popov, the famous Soviet clown, saw them. Dressed in his suit, red nose and all, he angrily threw the Christians out of the tent and escorted them off the grounds. Popov was the political officer for the circus.

The performers have returned to England several times since, and each time Mike and his co-workers have returned undaunted in their objective to reach them for Christ. Merv Knight with the Australians met the same circus on the other side of the world — "down under." The Aussies had specially printed literature for the occasion.

Decide on your approach. A clear objective will also help you develop a specific method for your outreach. In New Zealand, for example, one group of young Christians uses volleyball to accomplish their mission. Their goal is to invite Russian seamen to a church campground where they will be exposed to the gospel.

At the port of Lyttelton near Christchurch, one of the Christians who lives on a hill overlooking the harbor alerts the others when the Russian ships arrive. The young people drive up to the fishing vessels and go aboard with volleyball in hand ready to play with the crew. The ball is tethered at the end of a rope so it will not roll overboard. Sometimes these New Zealand Christians play dominos with the sailors.

After a few days of sports and fellowship aboard the ships, the young Christians take their hosts in groups of fifteen or twenty up to their church campground where the men can relax and play more volleyball or enjoy stiff competition in basketball or football. Occasionally they take the sailors horseback riding.

Meanwhile, a table is set up in the camp dining hall where the sailors can help themselves to Christian literature in Russian. The guests eagerly stuff the literature — New Testaments, Bibles, tracts — in their bags and carry them back to their ships.

The women sailors are taken to Christian homes. Seeing the children, they race with each other to pick them up and carry them around the house. This seems to ease the ache of not seeing their own. Deep friendships develop as Christian families begin learning Russian to be more effective missionaries to these sailors.

After some time working along the coast in this manner, it became easier for the Christian workers to walk onto the ships. They grew to know the sailors by their first names. And each time the Russians arrived in port, they would come looking for the Christians.

Know the right time. Timing is vital in building a strategy as well. Knowing when to fish is as important as where if you're going to be a successful "fisher of men."

David N. was a marine engineer, involved in developing marine propulsion units. His family took their holidays in harbor areas to get away from the telephone. So they knew exactly where the little fishing boats and the fishermen who had gone ashore would be. They also knew the time of year when the largest number of factory ships would be in the water around Scotland tracking the movement of the mackerel.

The factory ships depend upon the Scottish trawlers to supply them with their quota of fish each month. If the weather is too stormy for the Scottish fishermen, they can't supply the ships. This means there's no work on the factory vessels. When this happens, the crews come ashore.

"So when the trawlermen can't fish," David N. says, "we can do our fishing; we can be 'fishers of men'."

"Commuter missionaries" face a different challenge with timing when distributing gospel literature in train stations. Often guards attempt to hinder their work. Usually one team member will act as a lookout while the others give out the Scriptures.

"We have had some close calls," David T. recalls. "If it is difficult to enter the train, we wait until it starts to leave. We stand in the front row of people beside the train, and when everybody begins kissing and waving, we hold the Bibles up to show the people inside. In a flash, they open their windows, and we quickly put the Bibles inside."

Calculate the risks. In some of our work, much of the risk doesn't come from the people you are trying to contact; it often comes from the authorities in so-called free nations. Even in the heartland, Bible belt of America.

During the Czech concert in Bartlesville, we were not breaking any laws, but I'm sure the authorities would not have been happy had they known we were in the orchestra pit putting Scripture booklets on the instruments or distributing religious literature to the troupe back stage.

Wherever your gospel outreach is planned, be aware of the risks so you won't become frustrated or disappointed and so you can plan to minimize the opposition.

As you analyze your approach, ask yourself, "What can possibly get in the way of my objective?" People whom you would ordinarily consider friendly can prove otherwise. Even fellow Christians who may not share your vision. We are waging an invisible war, a spiritual battle, and people who may be friendly socially often are not so spiritually and could jeopardize your work.

Paul writes, "If it is possible, as far as it depends on you, live at peace with everyone . . . "[5] Don't be hostile to those who oppose you; they are living in another world and don't understand what you're trying to do. Instead, plan how you can get around them in a smooth, non-abrasive way.

And don't allow the risks in your outreach to slow you down or cause you to be fearful. Rather, consider them as challenges to develop a strategy that will be successful.

Prepare thoroughly. During my sea and air invasions of Cuba, hundreds of thousands of Bible portions and other Christian literature either floated ashore or were scattered over towns and villages where multitudes could find and partake of the Bread of Life. But these gospel sorties would not have been successful had our invasion teams not prepared thoroughly for the missions.

I recall one operation. A fellow teacher and a few dedicated students met with me on Saturdays to

---

[5] Romans 12:18.

package gospel tracts, assembly-line fashion. We packed the literature, together with a straw and a stick of gum, in the bags and heat-sealed them.

The chewing gum, we decided, would attract children or others on the beach and induce them to open the package and then remove the literature. The straw would keep it afloat.

When the day arrived to begin our mission, we stuffed the 50,000 packets into big plastic trash bags and hauled them aboard a boat in Georgetown Harbor. Our captain, meanwhile, carefully planned his course and loaded provisions for our voyage.

On another occasion, I planned a night flight across Cuba to drop thousands of literature packets. My pilot brought the appropriate charts to my home, and we began to plan the mission — load, airspeed, distance, fuel. Careful preparation, we realized, would be required for success. Did we have enough literature? How could we be sure it would reach the target area? What strategy would be most effective in accomplishing our task? These and many other questions needed to be answered.

Night after night and day after day, I lived this mission. Sometimes waking up at two or three in the morning, I would go to the dining room where the big aeronautical chart was spread on the table. I would pray and plan, figuring even how I would open the back door of the plane we did not yet have.[6]

---

[6] For the full account of these and other missions to Cuba, see my book, *Missiles Over Cuba* (Living Sacrifice Books).

You may not find it necessary to plan so inten-
sively for your mission. Certainly reaching the Czech
dancers did not call for the elaborate preparations of
a literature invasion of Cuba. But let me encourage
you to prepare adequately for your outreach.

Working Your Plan

Whenever possible, work in groups of two or
more people. The Scripture establishes this principle
clearly. The writer of Ecclesiastes 4:9 records:

> Two are better than one, because they have
> a good return for their work.

Jesus followed this precept in sending out His
twelve disciples and later when He commissioned
seventy-two others to proclaim the kingdom of God.[7]
And the Book of Acts records that the Holy Spirit
continued the pattern in the ordination of Barnabas
and Saul:

> The two of them, sent on their way by the
> Holy Spirit, went down to Seleucia and sailed
> from there to Cyprus . . . John was with them as
> their helper. They traveled through the whole
> island until they came to Paphos . . .[8]

Approaching visitors from foreign lands is not
without its risks, as we have seen. You may sometimes encounter hostility or personal danger. The
writer of Ecclesiastes explains the wisdom of num-

---

[7] Mark 6:7; Luke 10:1.
[8] Acts 13:4-6.

bers. "If one falls down, his friend can help him up," he says. "Though one may be overpowered, two can defend themselves. A cord of three strands is not quickly broken."[9]

But there are other practical reasons for working in teams — prayer and moral support, the multiplication of effort, and cultural considerations. David N. summarizes:

"My wife Nancy and I always work in pairs because some of the nationalities are a little bit suspicious of a woman. She is of particular help to me in this area because she relates well to the Russian women. But Nancy has unromantically been used as a pack horse some of the time as she faithfully keeps me supplied with literature.

"For instance, we have two bags. When two boat loads of Russians or Bulgarians come in, we see between ninety and ninety-five people. To cope with that number of Scriptures you need two bags. And if another boat of another nationality then appears, you need somebody to go and get some Polish or some Romanian literature."

Praying for Your Plan

The best of plans conceived of human wisdom are useless. The psalmist observes, "Unless the Lord builds the house, its builders labor in vain."[10] In effect the psalmist was saying, "Unless the Lord designs

---

[9] Ecclesiastes 4:10,12.
[10] Psalm 127:1.

your strategy, your labors will be fruitless." Careful planning and diligent labor must be empowered by prayer.

I encourage you to pray in faith that God will guide you in developing a strategy for reaching your immediate area of influence for Christ. God has a plan. Prayer will enable you to discover the one He would open for you. But other special qualities are also needed when breaking into new territories.

Part 4

Qualities for Success

10

The Way
to Success

On dark rainy days, the English have a saying, "Only mad dogs and Englishmen would go out in this kind of weather." But on this particular cold and soaking wet morning, even the English were staying inside.

Except for about seventy Russians meandering up and down the streets of the seaport village looking in the shop windows, David and Nancy N. were the only locals to be seen. Unlike the fishermen who had abandoned their task to the storm, these "fishers of men" were "letting down their nets" for an eternal catch.

At times when we fish for the souls of men, we can truly understand the frustration of Simon Peter and his fellow fishermen. The Gospel of Luke records how on one occasion they had worked hard all night and didn't catch a thing. Imagine yourself among them washing the nets. Along comes Jesus and says, "Go out where it is deeper and let down your nets . . . "[1] In other words, "Don't give up; keep fishing."

David and his friend were experiencing a similar disappointment as they attempted to distribute gospel literature to the Russian seaman. The Russians were not accepting anything from them. The "fish" weren't biting.

Realizing the fishermen were probably being watched and so were afraid to take the literature, the Christian workers kept on the alert. Within moments they identified four political commissars keeping a vigilant eye on their crew. David recalls the incident:

"From their key positions, they could see what we were doing almost everywhere we went. So the spiritual game of chess began. We waited until they were in a certain position where we thought we could get between the commissars and the intimidated seamen. Then the watchers couldn't see if anything was passed.

"One young Russian, perhaps not even twenty, continuously walked backwards and forwards past us, which is generally a sign that he would take something if we could get it to him. He was wearing jeans and running shoes and a thin, light green jacket. His breath could be seen in the air as he crisscrossed us.

"Studying his movements, I stood in the middle of the pavement so I was between him and the people who could see. As he passed again, I reached into my

---

[1] Luke 5:4 (TLB).

bag and quickly offered him a small Gospel of John which he could easily hide."

The seaman looked fearfully at David as he handed him the Gospel and in a dramatic manner returned it. "I cannot take this!" the young man exclaimed loudly so everyone around would see his demonstration. Inconspicuously he pointed behind him with his thumb. "Commissarus . . . behind . . . behind," he whispered.

"I spotted the political officer dressed in sailor's gear in the crowd behind staring at us intently. I took the Gospel back from the seaman in full view of the commissar but while returning it, the young fisherman put his other hand down in front of his stomach, slightly turning his body so the officer couldn't see. He quickly opened and closed his fingers indicated this was the best way. As I took the other one back from his left hand, I slipped a second one in his right hand."

The fisherman quickly stuffed it in his shirt and spoke with a low voice. "Thank you very much. If I take this and commissarus see . . . boom, boom!" He put his fist in his hand to indicate that if he was caught with the Scripture on his ship, he would be beaten.

Fruitful witnessing certainly depends on your spiritual preparation and strategic planning. But other qualities also must point the way to success. Practical knowledge is vital. Skilled fishermen know where to fish and how to lure their catch.

Broaden Your Knowledge

Before you cast your net, try to know the backgrounds and traditions of those you are trying to reach and the potential risks they face in receiving the gospel. It is vital that you know how to share the Good News simply and clearly as well.

One of the best ways to broaden your knowledge about a ministry is to observe others who are successful in it.

As you read, perhaps your heart yearns to participate in such an outreach: *Oh that I could help feed the men, women and children from an atheistic, Communist background who are eagerly gathering at our tables in the West for spiritual bread.* You may never have this opportunity personally, but as you look around, you see countless other souls — individuals in your own community — who are hungering for the Bread of Life.

I encourage you to associate with those in your area who are successfully involved in sharing their faith in Christ and see how they do it. Find out what works for them. Decide how you can apply their approach to your witnessing endeavor.

"Working on the street and in the train stations," says Brian L., "you've got to be wise; you have to be discreet." These words of wisdom come from years of experience often gained through painful trial and error. Joining other dedicated Christian workers on the front lines of evangelism will expose you to insights unattainable otherwise.

Reading greatly broadens your base of information. Subscribe to major newspapers and news magazines. Keep abreast of local, national and international news. Perhaps you live in a port city. Check the schedules of commercial shipping companies to determine the arrivals of foreign vessels. By studying newspapers devoted to maritime trade, John R. and his co-workers discovered that in one month alone 189 Russian ships docked in the British Isles, and each month more than forty thousand Soviet seamen visit western Europe. If God is calling you to minister among the suffering peoples of the world, you must know where they are. As with the Czechoslovakian dance troupe who performed in my own home town, you may find them right in your own community.

I encourage you to read books as well. That's how I got a lot of my training. Whether you study evangelism or drama, math or music, God can adapt your reading to His work. Perhaps you are thinking, *That's ridiculous. I studied botany. How's God going to use that in sharing my faith?* Have you thought of the possibilities? A plant exhibition, for example, where people from various nations are gathering? Or an encounter with a neighbor at your local nursery? Your knowledge of botany could give you just the rapport you need to win a person to Christ.

Never underestimate what God can do with a book. While working among sailors in his home port, someone loaned John R. a book on Christian work in Communist countries. He recounts how the book changed his life:

"The owner of the book later became my wife! When we got married, we hardly knew each other, but we had a common interest in God's work for Communist countries. We started a prayer meeting in our home and began to travel to Eastern Europe with Christian Missions to the Communist World. A month later, we received a letter from a port missionary asking for help, and a new way to reach out was given to us."

Be Aware of the Risks

Awareness enables preparedness. Knowing your opposition and how to get around it is always vital. This was of primary concern in our strategy for reaching the Czech dance troupe. And it is a constant requirement of those who daily face the difficult challenges of reaching oppressed people for Christ.

Perhaps the most critical need for awareness is the threat of persecution which visitors from afflicted lands face in receiving the gospel. Even with glasnost, Soviet travelers and visitors from other Communist lands frequently fear their superiors. In many countries, becoming a Christian could cost them their jobs and severe family hardship. In Muslim countries where we work, Christians are hung by the neck. Sensitivity to their risk is vital if you are to be successful in your approach. Your body language must not convey the feeling that you are offering them something dangerous. Often you can distribute gospel literature openly. Other times you may need a different strategy.

The almost-always-present Communist political officers are usually dressed the same as their crews. Yet, they have an air of officialdom that can easily be detected. It's a bit like a thief recognizing a policeman. After awhile you have a built-in instinct that tells you, "This guy's trouble." David N. tells how he and his team handle the officials:

"We always leave the political officers till last. If possible, we give them Bibles with a different color binder. This way they won't have a color reference if they should see a sailor with a Bible."

On one occasion, a political officer and his photographer positioned themselves on a jetty for several hours watching David and his team distribute Bibles to the sailors. Neatly dressed in a clean, canvas jacket and new-looking, knee-length leather boots, the dark-haired investigator stood with ominous poise.

"None of the seamen would take anything from us while he was there," David recalls. "He continued to stare piercingly at us while his friend took photographs to intimidate the seamen. Then the Lord sent His innovative light. We realized that these gospels were almost exactly the same size as the fun-sized Mars candy bars which my wife Nancy carried in her purse. The candy wrapper was even the same color as the Gospels!

"Our spy was boldly checking people to see what they got. Whenever a nervous seaman would refuse a Bible, we gave him a Mars bar. While the political officer checked the sailors who held up their candy bars for him, some of the seamen stuffed a Gospel into their pockets."

Finally, the officer tired of checking the sailors and left. The photographer remained and continued snapping photos with his telephoto lens.

"Our son Michael was with us," David smiles. "While we kept our best side toward the photographer, Michael went to the car and took out our camera with an old-fashioned 300mm telephoto lens which looked like a bazooka. Returning to the dock, he pointed this big cannon at him and took a few photos. It wasn't long until the mysterious photographer was gone. We found this to be an effective way to get rid of this sort of surveillance."

Risks can take many forms. Not always are you concerned about the ever-vigilant commissars whose job is to protect their charges from the "decadent" West. Sometimes local authorities create problems. David relates an incident which illustrates this:

"We were parked in a small Scottish fishing village one afternoon, working mainly with the Russians and some East Germans on shore. Noticing that we were giving something to these Eastern Europeans, the village traffic warden tried to see what it was.

"We are experienced in dealing with legal officers. When we become aware that somebody is behind us, we always cover our bags and try to make it difficult for him to see what we are doing.

"Undaunted, the curious policeman watched and waited until our bags were empty and we had to go back to our car. This way he identified us and returned to the police station to report what he had found."

The officer on duty that day was a member of the church which David and his co-workers attended when they were in town. "Oh, that's all right," he assured the traffic warden. "You don't have to worry about them. They're giving out Bibles."

The warden, though he did not attend church, became supportive and gave David and his co-workers a free hand.

Violence or the threat of harm takes its toll on the missionary as well. The secret is not to let these dangers deter you.

John R. recalls a painful encounter. "Once a drunken man at the bus station became angry and hit me in the mouth, breaking several of my teeth. I learned an important lesson, stand further back!"

On another occasion Tom V. H. talked to a Pakistani seaman for a half hour about life, death and eternity. The sailor appeared uninterested and finally left the room. Later as Tom attempted to leave the ship, the seaman was standing at the gangway with a long sword waiting to cut off his head. Tom recalls what happened next:

"The Lord took away my fear as I walked toward him. Suddenly an alert watchman, whom I knew to be a Christian, showed up and took away the sailor's sword. After I got home, my knees began to shake."

Of course the hazards of sharing your faith can have their humorous moments, as John R. can certainly tell you:

"To me it's more enjoyable to share the gospel than to visit with friends, but sometimes 'enjoyable' takes on a different meaning. One evening a young drunk fell down on the street in front of us. We stopped our sharing at the train station and put him in Tony's car. As we were driving him home, the drunk fell forward banging his head on the window. So Peter sat behind him holding his head straight. The still unconscious man began to vomit and Tony, still driving, was covered. Peter cried out as the man awoke then turned back to look at us. So we got the next heave. When we finally got him home to his family, they laughed at us."

Know How to Share the Gospel

Ivan Plett, a former prisoner from the USSR said, "You can't expect people who have been brought up in atheism all these years to come to conversion in a moment. The whole plan of salvation has to be explained to them."

But sharing your faith in Jesus Christ is not a complicated task. You do not need a theological degree to present the plan of salvation. The best qualifications for leading someone to Christ is a loving heart, a Spirit-filled life, and an understanding of how to present the gospel simply and clearly.

Billy J. was driving on the dock in Dublin with a list of arriving ships when he noticed a Cuban vessel.

Pulling up beside it, he bowed his head. "Lord, who do You want me to speak to today?"

A sailor beside the ship strolled up to his car and pushed his head through the open window. "Did you bring me the Bible?" Billy remembered seeing the man earlier in the day and promising to bring him a Spanish Bible which he had at home.

Billy shook his head. "I haven't had a chance to go home and get it."

The balding seaman leaned further into the car and pleaded, "Will you bring me a Bible?" He paused. "And come when it's dark, and make sure that it's wrapped up in a dirty paper bag."

The man quickly gave Billy directions for finding his way around the ship. "And when you come back, go directly to my cabin." Hardly waiting for a reply, he pulled his head out and walked away.

Walking up the gangplank later that night with the package, Billy surveyed the huge vessel. It was the first Cuban ship he had met. A lone crewman who couldn't speak English stood at the far end of the passageway. No one else seemed to be on duty. Billy quickly made his way up to the awaiting sailor's cabin and knocked.

Delighted when Billy handed him two Bibles, the seaman graciously invited him into the neat but dingy quarters. He motioned Billy toward the chair beside a little writing desk, then sat on a small bed nearby. Billy recalls:

"I learned that he was the ship's radio officer. He shared with me that he was searching for God. He didn't know who to ask in Cuba because he couldn't trust anyone. Speaking openly about God is to risk arrest."

Describing conditions in Cuba, the officer stopped seemingly to search for some special words. Then he looked expectantly into Billy's eyes. "We have been praying to God and we feel you've been sent from God."

Billy began to share the gospel with the seaman. "It's nice to know about God, but it's good to know that you have a personal relationship with Jesus . . . "

The officer leaned forward on the bed. "How can I do this?"

Using a Spanish Bible, Billy turned to the Gospel of John and slowly read through several verses. "The Word of God says you must be born again," he explained. "And if you ask Christ into your life, He will come in." Turning to Romans 10:13, he read the verse in Spanish, "Everyone who calls on the name of the Lord will be saved."

At the end of Billy's simple presentation of the gospel, the officer stood to his feet excitedly. "I want Christ." With Billy's help, he received Christ then prayed for his crew and for his family back in Cuba.

If you share your faith in Christ as a lifestyle, no doubt you have encountered many obstacles. Resistance to the gospel is inevitable. Nationality and cultural differences present challenges. But language is perhaps the most common barrier to directly sharing the gospel with the visitors from the East.

Identifying the nationality is vital. David N. shares insight here:

"Sometimes we have had as many as 150 people arrive in boats at the gate at the same time. They are surprised to hear you speak in their language. But the real secret of this contact is to get their nationality right the first time. So we watch the boats and take particular note of what they're wearing.

"We know from experience how to identify nationalities. You'll get one or two Russians who don't wear the typical clothing. They're splashed out in a Western ski jacket or something bright. Even when everyone is dressed in uniform, it can be difficult to place them.

"Because there are so many nationalities in the Russian boats, we've learned never to call a seaman *Russian.* He may not like to be called Russian. So we say, 'Excuse me, are you a Soviet?' Then when he says yes, we offer him a Bible. If we called a Polish man a Russian, he might accept a Bible but would feel insulted. If we got his nationality wrong again, we wouldn't be able to give him anything. You have to get his identity right the first time."

Knowing which language is spoken and learning expressions in that vernacular opens many doors of opportunity. Sometimes all you need to say is "Bibel" or "Biblia." The word, in one form or another, is universal. The problem is to convince the people that you would actually give them a copy free. Learning their word for "present" or "gift" provides ready acceptance. Before the Czechoslovakian dance troupe came to Bartlesville, for example, I called a friend whose father could speak Czech. The father lived in Chicago. Over the telephone, we taped the phrase, "This is a free gift for you," which we planned to say when distributing our literature. By the time these Czechs hit town, we had the words down. And they warmly received our gifts.

Our Mission workers have found another approach successful as well. Since some of them do not speak the languages of the visitors, they frequently slip printed material pointing the way to Christ inside the Bibles or Gospel portions. From these inserts, the visitors not only learn the plan of salvation but are shown how to pray and receive Christ.

Answering objections also opens doors to sharing. A Russian captain named Vladimir knew a little English and was friendly each time Alan C. and he met. On one occasion in English and halting Russian, Alan talked to Vladimir about sin. Holding out his hands, the captain protested proudly. "Our men are at sea for three months. No drink, no smoking, no women . . . no sin."

From the book of Matthew, Alan explained how Jesus described sin as coming from the heart. "Out of the heart come evil thoughts, murder, adultery, sexual immorality, theft, false testimony, slander. These are what make a man 'unclean' . . . "[2] Vladimir listened without further argument and willingly took a New Testament from Alan.

---

[2] Matthew 15:19,20.

Books dealing with science and creation are popular with Russians. Science and the theory of evolution have been well used by the Communists and others to destroy the spiritual worth of man. With their enlightened society then taught to act as beasts relying on sexual and material impulses, Russian leaders are mystified and now frustratingly plead in their newspapers for a "new morality." Often the Christian worker faces the conflict between science and faith as he shares Christ. Mike L. encountered such an argument as he witnessed to a Russian captain whose ship was visiting an English port.

"Scientists have proven that the world came into being through an explosion of gas in space," the captain contended.

Mike responded skillfully. "But who made the gases in the first place?"

"Well, it just happened."

"Captain, the world is delicately balanced upon an axis from which the slightest deviation would result in destruction. Could this just happen?"

Without waiting for his answer, Mike pressed further. "Can you believe that your ship was produced by an explosion inside a casual heap of metal, timber, plastic and wire? Captain, it takes more faith to believe your theory than to accept that the world was planned and created by God."

The officer finally accepted a Bible from Mike and invited him to visit the ship again the next time it was in port.

Spiritual preparation, strategic planning and practical knowledge, we have seen, point the way to effective evangelism. But all of these wither on the vine without motivation. Something or Someone must move us.

11

Keeping Your Motivation High

I have spent many hours on international flights. Sitting for so long in one position, my arms and legs grow stiff. Even sitting becomes painful. I am always glad when the plane taxis up to the gate at my destination, and I can disembark. Usually, it takes a little stretching to limber my muscles.

My experiences with stiffness on planes remind me of four leprous men in the Bible. Under siege by the mighty Syrian army, the lepers and the population of Samaria were starving to death.

The men faced certain death whether they stayed where they were or confronted the enemy. With this realization, they rose to their feet and boldly declared, "Why do we sit here until we die?"[1]

At dusk these physically harrowed men rose and advanced with determination into enemy territory. Meanwhile, the Lord had caused the Syrians to hear

---

[1] 2 Kings 7:3 (NASB).

the sounds of a great marching army, and they fled in panic. By the time the lepers arrived, the Syrian tents were deserted. Overjoyed, the men ate their fill, plundered the enemy, then returned to Samaria with the good news.

Sadly, many Christians are experts at sitting. They sit piously in their pews while the enemy lays siege to their communities; they sit idly in their homes while the world ensnares their families; they sit complacently in their careers while the sameness of life etches its despair deeper into their souls. Almost imperceptibly the strange numbness creeps into their lives. Their spiritual blood is not flowing; their circulation has stopped; they seek no personal ministry. Instead, they search for an answer to their mysterious disease through social endeavors. But to no avail.

Perhaps you have found yourself sitting, gradually doing less and less for the Lord. Your enthusiasm has waned, and your joy and excitement for Christ has faded.

The apostle Paul realized how susceptible we all are to losing our zeal. He writes, "Let us not become weary in doing good, for at the proper time we will reap a harvest if we do not give up." [2]

Have you ever wondered how you can keep motivated when things go wrong in your ministry or when you don't see the results you expect? Perhaps you have asked yourself, "How can I keep going even if I feel tired and disheartened?"

---

[2] Galatians 6:9.

Motivation is a vital mark of success in effective witnessing. Wherever you share your faith in Christ — in the seaports, train and bus depots, and truck stops of the world, or among your friends and loved ones in your own community — this quality is an enviable companion.

Let me offer some suggestions to help you keep your motivation high.

Work With Eternity in Mind

My greatest incentive for ministry comes from a sense of eternity. I know of no greater goal than to fulfill God's eternal purpose for my life. Jesus says, "This is to my Father's glory, that you bear much fruit . . . fruit that lasts."[3] When I introduce others to Christ's love, the results are everlasting.

The prophet Daniel writes, "Those who are wise will shine like the brightness of the heavens, and those who lead many to righteousness, like the stars for ever and ever."[4] Realizing that the results of my work will never end gives me the strength to continue when hardships and discouragements threaten.

John R. shares how this principle works in his life:

"I was standing on a campsite in Stuttgart. Inside our tents, the other members of our weary team were resting after driving all day. We were returning to

---

[3] John 15:8,16.
[4] Daniel 12:3.

England after a fruitful summer of visiting Christians in Eastern Europe.

"I thought back to one time during the summer when a Canadian colleague, Ray, had invited me to go with him to give out evangelistic literature to Eastern European truck drivers parked near our base. As we offered a few copies of John's Gospel to these men, they eagerly accepted.

"Suddenly, the Lord spoke to me as I surveyed the camp. He opened my eyes to something which had been there all the time but which I hadn't seen before. The campsite was full of visitors — Hungarians, Poles and Romanians — enjoying a holiday. Pushing away my tiredness, I quickly gathered up a selection of literature from the boxes in our car and set off round the campsite offering the Word of Life and a few words of testimony. Many campers gladly took the books.

"The next day I returned to England still tired but challenged by what I had seen. Reaching people from spiritually hungry lands as they come out to our territories was a new concept to me.

"I described the new mission field to our group at Christian Missions to the Communist World. We agreed that the Lord would have us reach this 'fruit.' Since then, who knows how many eternal decisions have resulted from our work among tourists and truckers?"

Setting your eyes on the everlasting fruits of your work will keep your motivation strong no matter

More than 6,000 Soviet fishermen and women arrive in their lifeboats in one season. We wait for them.

how hard the enemy struggles to dampen your spirit or render your efforts ineffective.

Take Courage in Success

Of course, success is a great motivator, too. Remembering past victories will help you keep going during the less exciting times in your ministry.

In my work, for instance, things go along pretty much the same. Often many day-to-day concerns seem to clutter my efforts. Some times my plans don't go smoothly. I'm sure you have experienced similar frustrations.

But several times a year I see incredible breakthroughs. Keeping these successes in mind helps me through the ordinary and sometimes discouraging days.

Tucking triumphs into your memories will give you courage. Imagine how you would have felt had you been with David N. one dull, cloudy day.

The seamen were wearing overalls and jackets against the cold. As a launch slid up to the pier, David identified it as a Bulgarian vessel by the green, red and white flag painted on its side. About forty men scrambled up the ladder onto the pier and fanned out around town.

David stopped one thin, sprightly sailor with dark skin and curly hair wearing blue overalls.

"Excuse me. Are you a Bulgarian?"

"Yes."

"Would you like a Bible?"

The man stopped abruptly, grabbed it from David's hand and quickly stuffed it into his overalls. But he missed his pocket and a bulge slid down his trouser leg and dropped onto the pavement.

The sailor grabbed the Bible when it hit the ground, abandoned his shopping bag, and bolted into a nearby shop. Before David could tell what was happening, the Bulgarian returned dragging a heavier, shorter man with him. Clapping his new Bible in his hands, the sailor shouted in English, "I believe the Bible!" He pulled his friend by the sleeve toward David.

The shorter man cautiously took the Bible the missionary offered. "Is this the whole gospel?"

David opened the front cover and let him count the books in the table of contents. The man's fingers moved down the column. Satisfied, he looked straight into David's eyes. "We are Christians from Bulgaria. We cannot get Bibles there." His voice broke, husky with emotion. "God has brought us from Bulgaria to Scotland to get this Bible."

David recalls another encouraging incident which occurred before the reunification of Germany. One day an inflatable launch docked at the pier. This time it was from an East German vessel. The sailors took many of the New Testaments David and his team offered them.

Later an East German official from the launch marched up to the missionaries. David took note of his sharp features. Smartly dressed in black, he clutched a briefcase in his left hand.

David offered him a New Testament. The man set his briefcase on the dock and glared.

"We don't need them on our ship! You are wasting our time. We've got a stack of these books." He held his hands apart, one above the other. "I'm the political officer, and we have collected so many of them."

David calculated the space between the officer's hands. Maybe enough for five or six books. Knowing his team had given seventy-five New Testaments to the men of the ship, David had to repress his joy. The missionaries had wondered whether the sailors had gotten the big red books onto their vessel without being noticed. The political officer had answered their question. That gave them the incentive to keep contacting East German sailors.

You may find it helpful to jot down the highlights of your own victories in a journal or notebook. This will enable you to remember how God is working in situations where you can see no fruit.

Don't Depend on Affirmation

Each of us needs affirmation. Compliments motivate us. Praise promotes a sense of well-being and accomplishment. But depending on the approval of others can be dangerous. Many Christians fly from project to project according to how much praise they receive and never find deep satisfaction and joy in their ministry. When we make commendation the basis for getting the job done, our ministry will lose momentum when criticism comes.

Sometimes we must forge ahead in ministry when others oppose. Noah is a notable example.

While building the ark, virtually everyone misunderstood his mission. Daily he suffered ridicule. But Noah patiently preached righteousness to the unheeding crowds. His persistent faith in spite of overwhelming opposition remains unsurpassed.

Suffering the taunts of unbelievers is tough enough. But when the opposition comes from fellow believers, the experience is even more painful. John R. recalls the struggles he and his team endured in beginning their ministry in Vienna:

"Over the past twenty years of sharing the gospel with the spiritually hungry from Communist lands, I have had few doubts or moments of depression. But one discouragement stands foremost in my mind. It came when Christians whom I respect misunderstood our mission. Some said we didn't use proper evangelism because we weren't bringing new converts together to form churches. Others thought our efforts were a waste of literature because 'the people won't read it.' A few told us that East Europeans wouldn't accept Bibles handed to them this way.

"It would have been easy to let these negative comments affect us. Instead, we went ahead with the work and saw tremendous results.

"Later, I had the privilege of showing these doubters that East Europeans were eager to receive Bibles and books. I took these Christians onto the street to see how relaxed and responsive these visitors to the West are. And how warmly the Easterners welcome our approach."

Let me suggest how you can maintain your enthusiasm when others criticize:

Keep a thankful attitude. What a privilege and honor it is to serve God. Paul writes, "We are Christ's ambassadors. God is using us to speak."[5] Imagine! We represent the King of kings. Whether we are misunderstood, disregarded or heaped with honors, the best praise will come from our Lord when we meet Him face-to-face. A grateful heart rejoices in this knowledge when even those close to us criticize or oppose our endeavors.

Maintain a positive and loving attitude. When you receive criticism, turn your bruised feelings over to God. Examine what others say about your work in the light of God's Word to determine whether their comments are justified. Then focus on God's calling. Be positive about your mission. Keep loving those who oppose you, even as Christ admonished in His Word: "Love your enemies and pray for those who persecute you."[6] Jesus is our example in this, for he experienced much criticism, even from His closest friends.

Cultivate a Sense of Humor

Impossible and discouraging situations can be made lighter with a bit of humor. Solomon said, "A cheerful heart has a continual feast."[7]

---

[5] 2 Corinthians 5:20 (TLB).
[6] Matthew 15:15.
[7] Proverbs 15:15 (NASB).

Brian L. tells of one cold, wet day when this principle helped him through some moments of distress.

"Tramping on the hard pavements in Vienna in icy weather can be tiring. The New Testaments and Gospels in the bag hanging around our necks drag heavily if filled with a lot of literature. Sometimes, we have to walk quite a ways before finding foreign contacts. To pass out books in poor weather, we stand under stairways that go down into underpasses. The wind and the rain whip along beside us. The only relief from the chilling cold is when we stop for refreshment on a bench in a little cafe.

"One particular day, I was out in the freezing cold putting Gospels on vehicles with foreign plates. I stuffed the literature into clear, plastic bags and slapped them onto the windscreens, feeling almost lost wading through piles of snow. There were many big holes in the ground, massive puddles frozen over with snow and ice.

"When I finished putting a Gospel on one truck and walked to another, the surface under me gave way with a crack. One leg went halfway down in water. Overbalanced with my bag, I slipped and fell. Water, diesel oil, snow and ice flowed around me, and I cut my face just above the eye.

"Slowly I pulled myself out of the hole, hobbled to my car, and drove off to look for friends working in the streets. Blood oozed from my head. I drove back through town but didn't see any of our group. After some time, I flagged down some friends who took me to the doctor.

"The doctor X-rayed my skull and stitched up my cuts. Then he left to examine the tests.

"A few minutes later, he came out into the hall and stood in front of us in his immaculate white coat. We waited for the verdict.

" 'You do not have to worry.' He spoke seriously in broken English. 'There is nothing in his head.'

"Suddenly, we all burst out laughing. His remark had put the situation into perspective. With chuckles, we thanked him and left, eager to return to our work the next day."

Seeing the humor in a tight situation can turn your attitude from one of despair to joy. Let the unexpected and funny incidents in your ministry help you laugh and enjoy the moment.

Keep Rejection in Perspective

A man was sitting in his car at the side of a busy street talking to his two small children. His car registration marked him as a diplomat from Albania, one of the most closed Communist countries of the world. A member of one of our teams tapped on the window, showing him a copy of *The Gospel of John* in Albanian.

The man rolled down his window, took the Bible and began to examine it carefully. He turned slowly through the pages while his children peered over his shoulder.

Meanwhile, the other team members silently prayed that he would keep the book and allow his children to read it. After a long time of studying, he handed the Gospel back through the window with a gesture of resignation. "I'm sorry. I am not permitted to be interested in this."

The missionaries walked away, still praying for him and his family. How angry they felt toward the atheistic system which grips his country and makes it life-threatening to learn about Jesus.

How do you react when you face rejection? Do you feel discouraged, maybe even want to quit? Don't let rejection dampen your enthusiasm.

In our years of ministry, we have learned that the most experienced and godly Christians can expect barriers of resistance in serving the Lord. How you handle these situations, however, will make the difference between fruitful service and defeat.

I want to share three practical ways to handle rejection:

Focus on what God has sent you to do. Setting your mind on the goal rather than the circumstance will help you attach less importance to how you are treated. It will help you remember that the battle is the Lord's, not yours alone.

Realize that not everyone is prepared to accept Christ's message. Imagine your mission field an orchard full of apples. On each tree you will find ripe and green fruit. Just as all the fruit in your orchard do not ripen at the same time, so some individuals will be ripe for spiritual harvest while others will not.

Whatever the case, be patient and let God use you as His instrument of love.

Remember that God does not hold you account-able for results, but for obedience. When you are faithful to what He has asked you to do, don't let rejection steal your joy. Instead, trust God to use even the darkest situations to bring about His desired results.

Every ministering Christian will experience rejection at some time. But those who do not let negative responses destroy their witness discover that God is more powerful than circumstances. And they experience the joy that God gives to those who obey — even when it would be easier to quit.

Maintain a Vision for the Lost

Unpleasant reactions to our witness are in-evitable. Each of us experiences rough times in min-istry. It's easy then to wonder whether our work is worthwhile. But the desire to see people come to know Jesus as their Savior keeps me going. I never tire of watching someone's face light up when he opens God's Word for the first time.

Maintaining a vision for the lost is the most essential ingredient in keeping motivated. To have a spiritual vision, we must love those who don't know Christ with God's love. We must see them through His eyes. We must value them as priceless people for whom Christ gave His life. Such a vision constrains us to "talk about Christ to all who will listen."[8] It

---

[8] Colossians 1:28 (TLB).

draws non-Christians to our message by the warmth and care they see in us.

Think also of the blessings enjoyed by those who turn to Christ. Their sins — past, present and future — are forgiven. They become children of God. They begin to experience God's peace and power in their lives. Indeed, the privileges of knowing Christ are boundless. How exciting to help someone discover them all!

Ask God to fill you every moment with His love for the lost — not just during the times you actively witness.

One of our team members took an afternoon off to visit an art gallery. He strolled through the immense halls for an hour, enjoying the Viennese culture. Looking out the window of the big building, he saw buses loading and unloading passengers. Suddenly the art, the culture, seemed worthless. He wanted to be with the people, reaching out to them with God's Word as they walked by.

With such a heart, God will open many doors for ministry to you. One day, a Hungarian lady was returning to her coach in Vienna. She carried enormous shopping bags full of oranges, apples, pears and bananas. She had bought as much fruit as she could carry since fresh produce is so expensive in Hungary.

Suddenly, her shopping bags burst open and the fruit rolled everywhere. Other Hungarians walking past didn't stop to help. Some even trampled her fruit.

A young man in our group bent down and helped her pick up the food, filling an extra bag he had on

ABOVE: Some of the missionaries of the Seaman's Christian Friends Society whom we help to supply with Bibles.

LEFT: Billy and Martha Jones, Dublin, Ireland, fervent witnesses for Jesus Christ.

hand. His genuine concern not only created a rapport with her, it also opened the door to talk to other Hungarians who had seen the incident.

As we have seen, practical knowledge and keeping motivated help build a fruitful, satisfying ministry. Other ingredients are also essential — boldness, determination and steadfastness. These characteristics will enable you to put your spiritual preparation and strategic planning to best use for the Lord.

12

Never Give Up

The Russian liner slipped into the pier at Dublin. Billy J. parked his car beside the huge white passenger ship and reached for his satchel in the back seat.

As he approached the vessel, one of the biggest KGB women he had ever seen was guarding the gangplank. She was six-feet-six-inches tall, very manly, with short black hair and a strong, heavy face. She proudly wore her KGB uniform with the red lapels.

Noticing Billy, she glowered. "Get off my ship!"

Billy didn't argue. He knew he couldn't get any Bibles on the liner right then, but he took note of the ship and of the woman guarding it. He and his wife Martha prayed for the men and women aboard.

The next year, the white cruise ship majestically pulled into the harbor. Again it carried the Russian "Olga."

After leaving his car, Billy saw her. Realizing she had plenty of time to get ready for him, he breathed a prayer. "Lord, show me how to reach her."

He strode straight up to her. "Olga, you were very rude to me last year. I only came bearing gifts." He showed her the "gifts." One was a beautifully illustrated children's Bible in Russian.

As Billy turned the pages and showed her the pictures, her face softened. Her big hands reached out and held the book. She said nothing for a few minutes, then asked to keep it.

Wise fishers of men understand that successful ministry takes perseverance. Reaching men and women for Christ often does not happen quickly and easily. Instead, it takes special qualities: boldness, determination and steadfastness to accomplish the work the Lord asks us to do.

Spirit-Inspired Boldness Changes Lives

Spiritual boldness is more than mere daring. It is stepping out in Christlikeness to conquer an area for God—sometimes without help from anyone else, maybe even without human encouragement, often when others disagree with you.

Such boldness begins with knowing who you are in Christ. He has given you all the resources you need to fearlessly proclaim His Good News. He has promised you unequalled victory. The apostle Paul explains, "In all these things we *overwhelmingly* conquer through Him who loved us."[1] Jesus will give you unlimited power to achieve this victory as Paul assures, "I can do all things through Him who

---

[1] Romans 8:37 (NASB).

strengthens me."[2] In Christ you can boldly go where He wants you to go and bravely do what He lays on your heart.

No doubt you have discovered that it's hard to be courageous when faced with difficult situations. The Russian liner made its final call to Dublin the next year after "Olga" accepted the children's Bible. Boarding the ship, Billy saw two officers guarding the entrance. Olga was gone. *Maybe they think two men equal one Olga*, he thought wryly.

Scowling, one officer stepped forward to block Billy. "What have you got?"

"Bibles." He gave each man a Bible. "I'd like permission to give each member of your crew a Bible."

While the Russians argued animatedly among themselves, a group of passengers walked by. Instinctively, Billy reached into his satchel, held up a Bible, and spoke loudly to the guards hoping the passengers would overhear. "This Russian Bible will change your life!"

One of the women immediately ran back. "You say Russian Biblia?"

"Certainly, madam."

"How much you vant for Russian Biblia?"

Billy handed her a Bible. "No money . . . free gift." She ran to show her friends who rushed over to see if they could get Bibles, too.

---

[2] Philippians 4:13 (NASB).

Still arguing loudly, the officers paid no attention. Two more women joined the group, then others came until a crowd of excited passengers had clustered around the open bags.

Before long, Billy had given away his entire stock of Bibles. The guards finally decided not to let the missionary on board. But he had already accomplished his goal.

Any of the courageous port missionaries will tell you that it is not easy to take Christian literature onto strange ships. Yet they have boldly persisted in the face of danger, persecution and stubborn resistance.

Such boldness changes lives. One seaman who visited Dublin, for instance, planned to commit suicide. Before he could carry out his intention, he discovered an old piece of paper he had stuffed in his pocket six months earlier. It was a tract telling how Jesus loved and died for him. That was the news he so desperately needed to hear. Right there, he accepted Christ as his Savior and received new life and hope.

Boldness is a work of the Holy Spirit. Only when we are filled with the Spirit can we step out bravely for Christ when we feel timid or afraid.

The Book of Acts records how Peter and John were imprisoned and threatened by the religious leaders of their community for teaching in the name of Jesus. The apostles had every reason to be afraid. But their Spirit-inspired boldness held them firm. "We cannot stop speaking what we have seen and heard."[3]

---

[3] Acts 4:20 (NASB).

No doubt you have been inspired by the bold-ness of the missionaries you've met in this book. Perhaps you have never experienced this power of God yourself. Your sword waves weakly for your Lord. But God wants you to open yourself to His power by asking Him in faith to fill you with boldness. He wants you to experience the ever-expanding, ex-citing ministry that comes when you walk closely with Him.

Determination Reveals Courage

Have you ever experienced a situation in which your fortitude melted away like soft butter on hot toast? Perhaps during a ministry crisis, you found little support from other Christians. Or didn't have enough money to cover all the projects you felt led to under-take. Or maybe you have worked for years without any acknowledgment or acclaim.

The Bible gives many examples of people who persevered for the Lord. The prophet Daniel displayed supernatural courage in the face of fierce opposition.

When the ruling authorities of his day ordered the people to quit worshipping God, Daniel deter-mined to pray openly. No one patted him on the back for his stand. No doubt some even mocked him as a fool. His determination to pray got him thrown into the lions' den. But in the end he triumphed when God shut the lions' mouths.

Jesus was the supreme example of determina-tion. The Bible records that He set His face toward Jerusalem though He knew death awaited Him and

even when His disciples tried to dissuade Him from
His mission.

That kind of persevering determination enables
us to find doors of opportunity we would otherwise
miss. Stan S. discovered this.

One Sunday afternoon, Stan and his co-worker
Andrew found a man reading on the gangway of a
large Cuban ship. The man was thrilled when they
offered him a Bible, a record and some booklets.
Seeing the chief officer, Andrew approached him
also. But he rejected the Bible.

"We would like to leave booklets and Bibles for
the crew," Stan explained.

The officer stared coldly at the missionaries.
"There are about thirty men on the ship. If you give
me the books, I will see that they get them."

Stan suspected that the officer would dispose of
the literature when they left. "But they are so bulky
and heavy," he offered kindly. "I'll put the books in
the messroom with your calendars."

The chief officer didn't like his suggestion. But
the port missionaries persisted. Finally, to get them
off his back, the officer allowed them inside. Three
seamen in the messroom gladly received the literature.

As Stan and Andrew went ashore, another man
called out. "Goodbye."

"I realized that he hadn't received a Bible," Stan
recalls. "Quickly opening my bag, I produced my last
two New Testaments. I glanced around for a way to

get them to him. Noticing a rope near him, I said, 'You can have these if you will throw me that rope.'"

The seaman quickly complied. "We tied the two Bibles and some literature to it and held our breath as he drew them up. In seconds, they were safely in his hands."

Then they heard a cry. A second sailor was perched on a plank, painting the stern. He wanted a Bible, too. "My heart rejoiced. The Lord had provided those two remaining New Testaments for those two men — and the way to get them across the gulf."

The rewards of determination are heartwarming. Jan V. tells of the extra effort it took him to get Bibles to some Soviet sailors.

"When it is difficult to get on a ship, I usually find a way — with the Lord's help — to distribute Bibles to the crew. I recall an incident in which I was able to reach a group of Russian seaman. I couldn't board any of the Soviet ships at first because they were guarded. But God had a different plan.

"I noticed a Dutchman with two Russian sailors returning from a shopping spree in a nearby village. From him I learned that more sailors were walking back from town.

"Rain began to fall heavily as I got in my car and started to look for them. On the way, I peered intently through the downpour. Finally, I saw them — eight seamen with their coat collars turned up, hands in their pockets, trudging along the road.

"I stopped the car, stepped outside and offered them Bibles. Not understanding English, a few looked puzzled. Then one realized what I had. Wiping the water off his face, he smiled and said something in Russian. Suddenly, all crowded around me wanting a Bible.

"Not speaking Russian, I got back in the car to keep from getting soaked as they examined the Bibles. I was amazed as I watched their reactions. Each man seemed fixed to his spot around my car, his back turned to the angle of the rain, water dripping off his clothes, Bible open.

"Even today, words cannot describe how I felt at that moment."

Determination does not quit in the face of discouragement, failure or setbacks. Many of our co-workers have experienced greater fruit by going back more than once. One of our teams, for example, approached a large Cuban ship four times. The first trip was on a dark evening. Two sailors were standing on top of the stairs and would not let the missionaries aboard. When offered Bibles, the Cubans waved their hands emphatically, "Not interested!" and promptly ushered the team back down the stairs.

Five minutes later, two of the missionaries went back with copies of Richard Wurmbrand's book, *Tortured for Christ.* Both the Cubans accepted this gift.

Their determination paid off. The next week, the missionaries went back again. After they distributed their literature, the political officer forced the crew to give back everything. But one sailor was able to slip some books into his back pockets. And the team returned once more to find even more success in giving away God's Word.

You may have to try more than once to accomplish the work God has laid on your heart. You may have to go it alone after others have become discouraged and quit. But one thing I have discovered: The Lord will certainly reward you for your determination in the face of obstacles.

Steadfastness Increases Strength

In Jesus' day, Roman soldiers wore hobnailed sandals that gripped any kind of terrain. When engaged in hand-to-hand battle on slippery soil, their footwear held firmly. On long marches over rugged ground, the shoes gave sure footing. Whatever his duties, the infantryman could perform his best because his sandals held their ground.

In His service, our Lord also expects us to stand firm. Paul urges, "Therefore, my beloved brethren, be steadfast, immovable, always abounding in the work of the Lord, knowing that your toil is not in vain in the Lord."[4] The apostle gives us three ingredients for steadfastness, (1) be immovable, (2) abound in God's work, and (3) know your work is not in vain. Let's look at each of these.

Be immovable. Having our goals and priorities set firmly will help us weather adverse situations.

Nancy N. is one who remains firm in her commitment to reach Eastern women with the gospel, even when her contacts are hostile.

---

[4] 1 Corinthians 15:58 (NASB).

She observes, "Women from Eastern Europe are much harder to reach than the men. Most women are difficult to spot among ordinary westerners because they don't dress like sailors and spend money on western cosmetics and clothes so they look like ordinary Scots. We really have to watch for things like someone carrying an older, larger handbag or little differences in dress.

"Most of the Eastern women do not speak or understand English either. Maybe for this reason, they usually say 'no' when offered literature.

"I've had some forceful 'nyets' from Russian ladies. Almost as if they were against you personally. Other times, they just don't understand what we are doing and are over cautious. But that doesn't make us quit trying to reach them. Sometimes we see victories when we least expect them."

On one occasion, two Russian women came ashore and split up. One passed Nancy and her co-worker. The Russian was quite tall, about thirty with dark hair. Nancy offered her a Bible, and she took it.

Immediately, she went into a shop and came back with her friend a few minutes later. The second woman was shorter, about forty-five, had plain features and wore an overcoat and leather boots. The first lady, with a mischievous look on her face, propelled her friend by the elbow around the corner. When she got almost level with me, she began talking rapidly, then became silent. She stepped back as though she wanted to look in the shop window.

A truck from the East rolls off a ship in England. The drivers all receive a welcome surprise!

On the streets of Vienna, curiosity and hunger are etched on the faces of men who have never seen a Bible.

We launch special scripture balloons deep into Albania. With borders opening, Albanian children run across a field to receive their first gospels.

In East Germany people swarm around the car of
Dr. Hans Braun. Five hundred books and three thousand tracts
were ripped out of the Christian's hands in twenty minutes.

*The Communist symbol
gone from the Romanian
flag. Who or what will
fill the hole?*

Bus passengers from the East are no longer interested in shopping. They sit in a Vienna park to read their first Bible.

Nancy spoke the only Russian phrase she knew, "This is a present," and handed the older woman a Bible. Thinking Nancy understood Russian, she took the book and began speaking in a stream.

"I had no idea what she was talking about. She hugged her Bible, overjoyed, almost in tears scarcely knowing what to do with herself. Out of the corner of my eye, I could see her friend chuckling."

When the woman with the Bible finally realized Nancy couldn't understand what she was saying, she simply said, "Leningrad," and put her hands together to indicate prayer.

"I assumed she meant she was a Christian from Leningrad," Nancy recalls. "She wanted to give us something so she began to hunt through her roomy handbag. Finally, she found a set of picture postcards of Leningrad dated from the 1970s which she handed to us."

A couple of days later, another team member, Alan, was with Nancy and her co-worker in the same place. He understands a little Russian. The same woman came ashore again, and he spoke to her. She smiled. Yes, she was a Christian from Leningrad. "She told Alan of her struggles working on the factory ship. But now she had met us and was thrilled with her Bible. How grateful I was that we were able to give her God's Word."

Abound in God's work. Our faithfulness grows in strength as we trust God to use us over a period of time.

Let me encourage you to read His Word daily and allow the Holy Spirit to apply the lessons in your ministry through exciting days and discouraging times. Bathe your work in prayer, and the Holy Spirit will enable you to continue producing fruit.

As you serve the Lord through the power of the Holy Spirit during good days and bad, your strength for the long-haul will increase. Circumstances will become less important, and the Lord will become dearer. Your determination and boldness will meld into steadfastness.

Know that your work is not in vain. Trust God for the results — even when it seems your efforts go unnoticed and unwanted.

Until glasnost most Soviet captains would not let port missionaries roam freely around their ships. They were taken to one area, such as an office or chief's cabin, and left there. For years, the missionaries worked in such limited capacity. But they didn't let discouragement stop them.

Then glasnost began to thaw the atmosphere. During this window in time, opportunities for distributing gospel literature have dramatically increased, and the sailors are more open. David and Nancy N. now joyfully report, "We don't have to follow the sailors, they follow us."

Billy J. recalls an encouraging incident. "One man said to me, 'What is so important about this book that we aren't allowed to have it?'

"I answered, 'This book will change your life.' And I went through the ABCs of the gospel with him.

He probably wouldn't have dared asked such a question a few years ago.

"Isaiah 55 says God's Word will not return void. The Bible truly is powerful and sharper than a two-edged sword. So I never hide the Word of God when I go out to distribute. In my Christian Seamen's uniform, I go directly up and tell the sailors who I am. I am trusting God to open doors and to use the literature in the hearts of the men I contact — even when I don't see the results."

God works even when we don't see the fruit. When I was in prison in Cuba, a major came into my cell screaming and yelling. His face was red, and he threatened me with all kinds of punishment. He threw down a plastic package, one of the pieces of literature our group had thrown into the sea before we crash-landed on the island. "Why have thousands of these come to our shore? People are passing them all around."

I could have gotten very discouraged wondering why God had let me get into this predicament since I was only trying to follow what I thought He wanted me to do. And the latest word was that I would be spending the next twenty-four years in a Cuban jail for my efforts to float Bibles to Cuban Christians.

Yet, this major gave me courage because I realized that God had directed the literature to the very people we had intended. It gave me the assurance that God was working when I couldn't see the results.

But opposition can dim our outlook and cause defeat. Many of the people who shared in this book told me that at times resistance seems like a personal attack. They think, *That person doesn't like my looks*, or *He dislikes my character.*

Then they remember that they are in the heart of an eternal battle. Satan would love to discourage them, to make them quit. That's when they draw on the reservoir of incredible strength which boldness, determination and steadfastness have built into their lives. They find courage that appears as an outward calmness that cannot be explained apart from God's power. With such strength they endure attacks from those to whom they minister; they withstand criticism from colleagues and Christian friends; and they persevere under intense pressure.

Our Lord has provided the same resources for us. Do you hear His incredible challenge to you? In this book you have been looking through the window in time which God has given us to reach men and women for Christ. Do you feel the urgency of the mission? Accept the challenge for His glory — and never give up.

Part 5

The Challenge

13

Let Down
Your Net

Psssstt!"

Mark J. peered upward at the two sailors barely visible in the dusk motioning to him from the bow of the Soviet cargo ship.

"Biblia! Biblia!"

The port missionary wondered how he was going to reach them with the Bibles. Moments earlier another seaman had raised the gangplank so Mark couldn't climb aboard. He was lingering alongside the ship when the sailors furtively called to him.

The light was fading rapidly. Mark considered tossing the Bibles upward, but that was out of the question; he couldn't risk them falling into the water. Suddenly, one of the men climbed over the railing and hung down the side while his companion held onto his legs. Mark climbed onto one of the large posts to which the ship was tied and stretched upward. Arms straining, no one speaking, missionary and seamen tried in vain to make contact. Finally the sailor retreated behind the railing. Motioning Mark to stay, the Russians disappeared. The missionary waited wonderingly.

Suddenly, a slight scraping noise caught his ear. In the twilight he could see a long wooden pole coming out over the rail. Dangling on the end was something like a small fish net. The determined sailors were pushing it out then down the side of the hull.

Mark dropped his precious cargo into the net, then watched the pole rapidly slide upward into the darkness . . .

If only we could capture this touching scene on the canvas of our hearts. As I travel the world and visit with some of the remarkable men and women whose stories you have read, I am captivated by their vision, challenged by their courage.

Hearing the Call

In this book you have witnessed what God can do when men and women capture the vision and dedicate themselves to the task of reaching their world for Christ. You have joined them aboard ships and walked beside them in fishing villages. You have mingled with them among the Eastern tourists at bus stops and train depots. You have followed them to the campsites of truckers. You have observed the overwhelming spiritual hunger. Deep inside you a voice has called. It is the voice of the Master. "Let down your net. I want you to fish for the souls of men."

Picture with me for a moment a scene long ago.

Pressed by a great crowd beside the seashore, the Master notices two empty boats at the water's edge. Beside them, fishermen are washing their nets. One of them is Simon Peter.

Stepping into Peter's boat, the Master asks him to push out a little into the water so He can speak to the people from there.

Later as the crowd begins to leave, the Master's attention turns to Peter and the other fishermen. He cannot help overhearing their mumbled conversations. The fish are not biting, and they are troubled. They have worked hard all night without even one fish to show for their efforts.

The Master calls. "Go out where it is deeper, Peter. Let down your nets *on the other side*, and you will catch lots of fish."

The fishermen grumble. But the Master is persistent, and they try again. This time their nets are so full they begin to tear. A shout for help brings other boats, and soon all are overflowing with fish and on the verge of sinking.

Awestricken, the fishermen return to shore with their catch. They had heard the Master's command to let down their nets. Now they learn their mission: "From now on, you will be fishing for the souls of men!"

Such is the Master's call and mission for each of us. I have found no experience in life more exciting and spiritually rewarding than the adventure of fishing for people. I am grateful for the fellowship of Christians who have a simple but profound understanding of the Lord's heart. And in this book, I have sought to enlarge your sense of mission. Do not be like so many of God's fishermen who are preoccupied with mending their nets, insisting that "fishing for men" is the task of special saints with a special "missionary call." The Master is calling *you*. When you begin to fill your net with people whom you introduce to Jesus Christ, you too will begin the most exciting, joyful, and rewarding adventure of your life.

A Lesson From Jonah

The first missionary God called to another culture was Jonah. You know the story. Jonah didn't like the people and was content to preach destruction to them. When Nineveh repented and turned to God, Jonah was furious. The only account we have of the end of this rebellious missionary was his argument with God for sparing the people. If God could call a bitter, negative, unwilling Jonah, how much more does He desire to send us, His Children of Light?

Many Christians are seemingly waiting for a mysterious call to take the gospel. Are we simply school teachers (as I have been several times), plumbers, construction workers, cashiers? If we don't hear the Master's call and fulfill our mission, will our money-making professions swallow us the way the whale swallowed Jonah?

If we do not "let down the net," will God mysteriously replace us with another fisherman? The sea of humanity is teaming with fish. Peter's boat could not contain the load. Other vessels raced to the rescue. Can we be sure that someone else will net our catch?

I have always been proud that for many decades more than 80 percent of the world's missionaries have come from North America. But recently I read a sobering report by Juan Toirac, a Cuban pastor now with the Lord. He said, "In the '60s there were approximately 60,000 foreign missionaries in the world. At present — when the population of the world is one-third larger, the spiritual needs greater, and the possibilities to reach spiritually hungry people unprecedented — the number of foreign missionaries has dropped to approximately 35,000. Many of the missionaries have been failing, defeated and forced to return home because the churches have not been praying.

"About one-fourth of the 35,000 missionaries that are supposed to be on the mission field are at home, floating from church to church seeking for additional support to return to the field. Many of them are in the States from one to three years without being able to secure enough funds to return to the field. Consequently, they become discouraged and stay home.

"In ten years, 20,000 to 35,000 foreign missionaries who are supposed to be in the field will be ready for retirement, and there will be no replacements. Reliable calculations are that in the next ten years only approximately 5,000 new foreign missionaries will go to the field of world missions."

God is looking for ordinary people like us who have open hearts and a vision for the world. Jesus says, "Go into all the world and preach the good news."[1] This commission was not given only to His first disciples. The examples and teachings of Christ, the works of the early church recorded in the Book of Acts, and the emphasis of the New Testament Epistles all bear witness that every Christian is called to man the nets.

Somehow we have gotten the idea that the early Christians were different from us. But Jesus chose common, ordinary, working people with weaknesses similar to ours. Many of them we have built into heroes. Yet the only difference between most of them and the majority of us is that they were obedient to their resurrected Lord and filled with His Holy Spirit. With these qualities, we could turn the world upside down and experience a mighty spiritual revolution like that in the first century.

Is the Window Closing?

No one can predict how long glasnost will last. Lenin encouraged glasnost in the 1920s by opening churches and encouraging Western investment. Stalin permitted a religious glasnost in the '40s during the war with Germany. Only time will reveal how long the current window of freedom will remain open.

The winds of change are blowing wildly across Eastern Europe. Desperate cries for freedom are

---

[1] Mark 16:15.

fermenting political upheaval and rekindling the fires of oppression.

Jesus cautions, "Do you not say, 'Four months more and then the harvest'? I tell you, open your eyes and look at the fields! They are ripe for harvest."[2] In these pages, we have peered through the window into the Communist world. We have seen the ripened fields. But one cannot help but ponder the creaking of the window closing against new winds of political persecution. I feel a great sense of urgency to complete our task.

Western Christians are tempted to focus less on the church in the East now that the Communist walls are crumbling. Failing to see the sacred drama emerging from decades of spiritual vacuum, many seem to be turning a deaf ear to the urgent call for Christian workers. In nearly twenty years of work with Cuba, I have been acutely aware of this. But today the need is dramatically greater. We dare not miss this unprecedented opportunity.

Unless you have seen the spiritual hunger with your own eyes, it is difficult to communicate the incredible sense that history is being made. After decades of living without God, it seems only natural to them to receive His free gift of love.

I'll never forget the look upon the faces of the Russian engineers on the factory fishing ship I visited as they received our gospel literature. They smiled and said they were atheists, the only answer they knew. Then they crowded around us and took every-

---

[2] John 4:35.

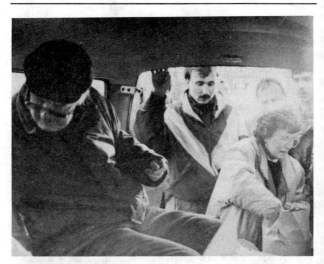

Nancy N. with the Rev. Trevor Manning (top) and fellow Christian workers (bottom) do not have to "follow" the Russians. Now the Russians follow them.

thing we had, asking for more. That one incident pours enough fire into me to last for another ten years.

Your Net Awaits You

The events in this book cover the 1970s, '80s and '90s. In those years we have seen dramatic changes in governments. But the spiritual hunger has not diminished. Rather, we are getting a glimpse of its intensity. Our nets are full. Each time we cast them into the waters, they nearly break with the fish who desire to jump in. Now the net is passed to you.

I encourage you to make a total, irrevocable commitment of your life to Christ. Be filled with His Holy Spirit. Study the world's need for Christ. Pray for the missionaries you've met in this book. Pray for the nations that have been liberated. Pray for the countries still struggling to break free. Ask God to keep them viewing on a spiritual plane. Ask the Lord to open the eyes of more Western Christians to the opportunities that await them. Ask the Lord to develop within you His eyes, His mind, His heart.

David N. says, "We have discovered that an average of 396 Eastern Europeans come to England everyday. We can help the church minister to this vast mission field which is just walking into our back yard. The Lord is saying to us, 'Look, put your nets out on the other side of the boat; you can do your evangelism here.' That's how the concept of letting down the nets fits itself into my life."

Begin sharing Christ as a way of life wherever you are — in your neighborhood, your campus or classroom, your office or factory. In the USA, there are several seaports, many tourists and numerous foreign students. Beginning at home, let God use you to spread His Word to the entire world through your prayers, your financial support and your personal involvement.

Perhaps, like the disciples, you will be called to leave the nets of your present involvements to follow Christ to a foreign mission field. Be prepared to go. Don't be afraid to offer yourself to God for service wherever He leads you.

My purpose in writing this book has not been to entertain. Instead, I have invited you to peer through a window in time at the dramatic landscape of spiritual harvest.

The testimonies you have read are no longer the sacred property of those who told them. They are now yours. Grab the ropes. Hear the Master's call. Cast your net with them.

For more information about the needs and ministry of Christian Missions to the Communist World and for additional copies of this book, please write:

In USA: C.M.C.W.
                P.O. Box 443
                Bartlesville, OK 74005
                USA

In Australia: C.M.C.W.
                P.O. Box 598
                Penrith NSW
                2751 Australia

In Canada: Klaas Brobbel
                J.T.T.C.W.
                P.O. Box 117 Port Credit
                Mississauga, Ontario
                Canada L5G 4L5

In England: Christian Missions
                P.O. Box 19
                Bromley Kent, BR1 1DJ
                England

In New Zealand: J.T.T.C.W.
                P.O. Box 69-158
                Glendene, Auckland 8
                New Zealand

 **Tom White** was imprisoned for seventeen months for smuggling gospel literature into Cuba. He is program coordinator for the USA office of Christian Missions to the Communist World and has been affiliated with the mission since 1972 when he began his smuggling activities.

Christian Missions to the Communist World has four main purposes:

1. To give Christians in Communist countries and in countries emerging from communism Bibles, Christian literature, and evangelical broadcasts in their own language.

2. To give relief to the families of Christian martyrs in these countries.

3. To bring to Christ, Communists in the free world.

4. To warn Christians in the West of the dangers of communism by informing them about the atrocities committed against our brethren in the faith in Communist countries.

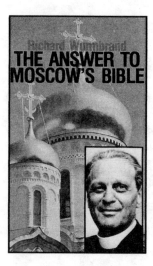

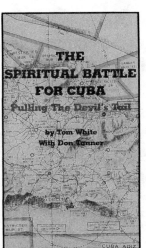

THE SPIRITUAL BATTLE FOR CUBA

by Tom White

Paperback — 170 Pages

---

*3.95

Subtitled: PULLING THE DEVIL'S TAIL

Tom White describes the struggling Cuban church entering the 1990's.

Police attacks on worship services. Communists won to Christ.

Secret printing presses. Balloon launches with Gospels from ships.

Documented accounts with photographs.

THE PASTOR'S WIFE

by Sabina Wurmbrand

Paperback — 218 Pages

*4.95

The story of a Christian mother who was separated from her 9-year-old son and sent to a slave labor camp, knowing that her husband was also imprisoned for his Christian work.

Battered and starved, she still managed to bring a ray of hope to those around by her remarkably strong faith in Christ.

"Some may even feel it surpasses anything her husband has yet written." — Church Times